40 Ways to Support Struggling Readers in Content Classrooms, Grades 6-12

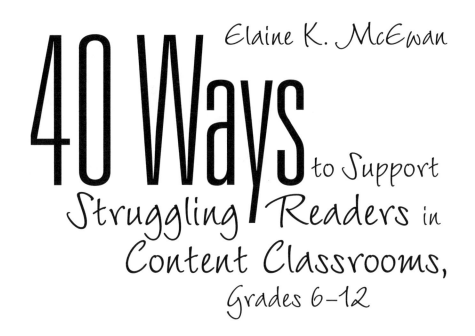

Elaine K. McEwan

40 Ways to Support Struggling Readers in Content Classrooms, Grades 6–12

A JOINT PUBLICATION

NATIONAL ASSOCIATION
OF SECONDARY SCHOOL
PRINCIPALS
promoting excellence in middle and high school leadership

CORWIN PRESS
A SAGE Publications Company
Thousand Oaks, CA 91320

For information:

Corwin Press
A Sage Publications Company
2455 Teller Road
Thousand Oaks, California 91320
www.corwinpress.com

Sage Publications India Pvt. Ltd.
B 1/I 1 Mohan Cooperative
Industrial Area
Mathura Road, New Delhi 110 044
India

Sage Publications Ltd.
1 Oliver's Yard
55 City Road
London EC1Y 1SP
United Kingdom

Sage Publications Asia-Pacific Pte. Ltd.
33 Pekin Street #02-01
Far East Square
Singapore 048763

Printed in the United States of America.

Library of Congress Cataloging-in-Publication Data

McEwan, Elaine K., 1941–
40 ways to support struggling readers in content classrooms, grades 6–12 / Elaine K. McEwan.
 p. cm.
Includes bibliographical references and index.
ISBN 978-1-4129-5205-7 (cloth)
ISBN 978-1-4129-5206-4 (pbk.)
 1. Reading (Secondary) 2. Reading—Remedial teaching. 3. Content area reading.
I. Title. II. Title: Forty ways to support struggling readers in content classrooms, grades 6–12.

LB1632.M347 2007
428.407′12—dc22

2006101119

This book is printed on acid-free paper.

07 08 09 10 11 10 9 8 7 6 5 4 3 2 1

Acquisitions Editor:	Robert D. Clouse
Editorial Assistant:	Jessica Wochna
Production Editor:	Melanie Birdsall
Typesetter:	C&M Digitals (P) Ltd.
Copy Editor:	Marilyn Power Scott
Proofreader:	Gail Fay
Cover Designer:	Rose Storey
Graphic Designer:	Lisa Riley

Table of Contents

Problem-Solution
Table of Contents

WHEN STUDENTS CAN'T RETAIN INFORMATION FOR THE TEST . . .

Topical
Table of Contents

SUMMARIZING

VOCABULARY INSTRUCTION

WRITING TO LEARN

List of Instructional Aids

Preface

The major challenge of teaching secondary content in the current era of accountability lies in helping *all* students read the massive textbooks, understand the complex concepts and ideas, and demonstrate proficiency on high-stakes tests.

No Child Left Behind (2002) has created a growing sense of urgency on the part of every secondary educator to find ways to help struggling readers achieve. The idea is not that you are expected to teach struggling readers *how to read.* However, you *are* increasingly being expected to teach the knowledge and skills related to your discipline on which all students will be tested. To reach even a modest level of proficiency, struggling readers need support. While this book doesn't provide easy answers, it contains dozens of ways that you can scaffold these frustrated students to enable them to be more successful in your classroom.

WHO IS THE STRUGGLING READER?

Struggling secondary readers *do* know how to read. They are not nonreaders. They just can't read the same quantity and difficulty of material found in their content textbooks as their on-grade-level peers. Struggling readers are usually below-grade-level readers. However, you will find some students on grade level who are temporarily struggling in certain disciplines or for certain topics (e.g., honors biology students using a college-level textbook).

Most struggling readers have a few gaps here and there in their phonics knowledge, making it difficult for them to identify multisyllabic content words without support. Others cannot identify words quickly enough to read fluently. There are still other struggling readers who can pronounce the words but don't know what they mean, because they lack the necessary background knowledge and vocabulary. Most struggling readers do little independent reading because it is a painful process, and their word and world knowledge is limited. When motivated and supported in content classrooms, struggling readers *can* master content as well as improve their reading and writing skills. Initially, the goal of scaffolding struggling readers in your content classroom may seem overwhelming and unrealistic. It is, undeniably, a challenge. However, do not let the enormity of the task deter you from experimenting with one or two of the research-based and classroom-tested approaches found in this book. *Start modestly and aim for short-term success.*

WHO THIS BOOK IS FOR

I have written *40 Ways to Support Struggling Readers in Content Classrooms, Grades 6–12* specifically for academic-content teachers (social studies, science, mathematics, and English) who want to become more adept at meeting the needs of students who struggle with mastering academic standards and content in their classrooms. The following audiences will also find the book to be helpful:

- Literacy coaches, interventionists, teachers of English language learners (ELLs), as well as Title I and special education teachers who support secondary teachers in meeting the needs of at-risk students
- Secondary administrators and department chairpersons who mentor, coach, and evaluate teachers, both novice and experienced
- Teams and departments who desire to choose one or more of the 40 ways to develop content-specific lessons that incorporate the techniques
- Central office administrators who provide professional development for secondary teachers
- University professors who teach courses focused on reading in the content areas

OVERVIEW OF THE CONTENTS

40 Ways to Support Struggling Readers in Content Classrooms, Grades 6–12 is about scaffolding—the process by which expert teachers support novice learners. Providing academic scaffolding for struggling readers is like throwing a life preserver to beginning swimmers floundering in the deep end of the pool. Even though you may not be able to teach them all they need to know to be highly proficient swimmers (readers), you can save them from drowning (failing) in the deep water.

The book contains 40 research-based and classroom-tested activities that teachers can implement to help struggling readers be more successful. An additional benefit of many of these methods is that they also have the potential to raise the achievement of average and above-average students.

The 40 activities are arranged in numerical order from 1 to 40. They can be accessed through three separate tables of contents found at the beginning of the book:

1. A traditional table of contents in which the various methods are listed in numerical order followed by the appropriate page numbers

2. A problem-solution table of contents in which the various methods are grouped as solutions to these common problems:
   - Students who read it but don't get it
   - Students who don't get it, even after you've taught it
   - ELLs and other students who lack vocabulary
   - Students who are overwhelmed by too many concepts
   - Students who lack background knowledge about academic content
   - Students who can't read the textbook at all
   - Students who are bored, unmotivated, or sleeping in class
   - Students who are confused
   - Students who need to process what they are hearing and reading more frequently
   - Students who can't retain information for tests

3. A topical table of contents in which the various methods are grouped by categories (e.g., Cognitive Strategy Instruction, Graphic Organizing, Vocabulary Instruction)

Each of the 40 activities contains the following features:

   - An intriguing *quotation* or *definition* to grab your attention
   - A brief *description of the method* and suggestions for how to implement it
   - *Recommended resources* to help you gain a more in-depth understanding of the method, either through independent study or as part of a professional learning community
   - *Research citations* that demonstrate the power of the method to get results
   - Accompanying *instructional aids* where applicable

You do not need to read this book from beginning to end to benefit from its contents. Skim one or more of the three tables of contents and select an approach, a problem, or a topic that appeals to you. Each of the 40 activities can be used singly. However, many of the approaches gain power when used in combination with one another. You will find cross-references and advance organizers throughout the book to help you make connections between various approaches.

QUESTION THE AUTHOR

One of the ways described in this book for improving students' understanding of text is Activity 7, Teach Students How to Question the Author. This approach suggests that you explicitly teach your students how to question the author of any text that they read—conducting an imaginary dialogue, if you will. I engage in a similar exercise when I am writing books: I imagine conversations with you, the reader, and try to answer your questions and address your concerns as they might occur during your reading. There are several questions and reactions that content teachers typically have when they hear about some of these approaches for the first time:

I can't possibly do all these things in addition to what I'm already doing.

Please remember that this book provides options, not mandates. Consider these approaches as possibilities, not prescriptions.

These ideas are great, but I don't have the time. I have content to teach.

The underlying premise of the 40 ways is to help you teach more in less time—not make more work for you. Although an initial investment of time is required to learn a new approach, the payoff in increased student achievement will be worth it.

I am only one person. How can I teach content and help the students who can't read at the same time?

I am suggesting that you support struggling readers, not teach them to read from scratch. That is someone else's job.

Acknowledgments

I am grateful to the many middle and high school teachers and principals who have continued to ask the tough questions and been persistent about finding ways to support struggling readers in their classrooms. They have motivated me to find answers in the fields of reading, cognitive science, and educational psychology. Special thanks go to Allyson Burnett (interventionist at Alief Hasting High School, Houston, TX), Raymond Lowery (associate principal for instruction at Alief Hastings High School, Houston, TX), Val Bresnahan (special and regular education teacher at Franklin Middle School, Wheaton, IL), Beth Balkus (principal, Millard Central Middle School, Omaha, NE), and Linda Nielsen (reading teacher at Pacifica High School, Oxnard, CA).

As always I thank my husband, Raymond, for his love, encouragement, *and* copy editing. We slipped this book into an already full schedule, and he rose to the occasion. He tells the truth in love with a tender heart and a patient voice. No writer could ask for a more supportive partner.

Corwin Press gratefully acknowledges the contributions of the following people:

Dr. Scott Mandel
Corwin Press Author
Teacher
Los Angeles Unified School District
Los Angeles, CA

Carl A. Young
Assistant Professor, Curriculum
    and Instruction
North Carolina State University
Raleigh, NC

Barbara L. Townsend
Reading Specialist
Elkhorn Area School District
Elkhorn, WI

Shari Hills Conditt
National Board Certified Teacher,
    History
Woodland High School
Woodland, WA

About the Author

 **Elaine K. McEwan** is a partner and educational consultant with The McEwan-Adkins Group, offering workshops in leadership and raising student achievement, K–12. A former teacher, librarian, principal, and assistant superintendent for instruction in a suburban Chicago school district, she is the author of more than 35 books for parents and educators. Her Corwin Press titles include *Leading Your Team to Excellence: Making Quality Decisions* (1997); *The Principal's Guide to Attention Deficit Hyperactivity Disorder* (1998); *How to Deal With Parents Who Are Angry, Troubled, Afraid, or Just Plain Crazy* (1998); *The Principal's Guide to Raising Reading Achievement* (1998); *Counseling Tips for Elementary School Principals* (1999) with Jeffrey A. Kottler; *Managing Unmanageable Students: Practical Solutions for Educators* (2000) with Mary Damer; *The Principal's Guide to Raising Math Achievement* (2000); *Raising Reading Achievement in Middle and High Schools: Five Simple-to-Follow Strategies for Principals* (2001); *10 Traits of Highly Effective Teachers: How to Hire, Mentor, and Coach Successful Teachers* (2001); *Teach Them ALL to Read: Catching the Kids Who Fall Through the Cracks* (2002); *7 Steps to Effective Instructional Leadership, Second Edition* (2003); *Making Sense of Research: What's Good, What's Not, and How to Tell the Difference* (2003) with Patrick J. McEwan; *10 Traits of Highly Effective Principals: From Good to Great Performance* (2003); *7 Strategies of Highly Effective Readers: Using Cognitive Research to Boost K–8 Achievement* (2004); *How to Deal With Parents Who Are Angry, Troubled, Afraid or Just Plain Crazy, Second Edition* (2004); *How to Deal With Teachers Who Are Angry, Troubled, Exhausted, or Just Plain Confused* (2005); *How to Survive and Thrive in the First Three Weeks of School* (2006); and *Raising Reading Achievement in Middle and High Schools, Second Edition* (2007).

Elaine was honored by the Illinois Principals Association as an outstanding instructional leader by the Illinois State Board of Education with an Award of Excellence in the Those Who Excel Program, and by the National Association of Elementary School Principals as the National Distinguished Principal from Illinois for 1991. She received her undergraduate degree in education from Wheaton College and advanced degrees in library science (MA) and educational administration (EdD) from Northern Illinois University. She lives with her husband and business partner E. Raymond Adkins in Oro Valley, Arizona.

Visit Elaine's Web site at www.elainemcewan.com where you can learn more about her writing and workshops or contact her directly at emcewan @elainemcewan.com.

Teach the Seven Strategies of Highly Effective Readers

To assume that one can simply have students memorize and routinely execute a set of strategies is to misconceive the nature of strategic processing or executive control. Such rote applications of these procedures represents, in essence, a true oxymoron—nonstrategic strategic processing.

—Alexander and Murphy (1998, p. 33)

If the struggling readers in your content classroom routinely miss the point when "reading" content text, consider teaching them one or more of the seven cognitive strategies of highly effective readers. Cognitive strategies are the mental processes used by skilled readers to extract and construct meaning from text and to create knowledge structures in long-term memory. When these strategies are directly taught to and modeled for struggling readers, their comprehension and retention improve.

Struggling students often mistakenly believe they are reading when they are actually engaged in what researchers call *mindless reading* (Schooler, Reichle, & Halpern, 2004), zoning out while staring at the printed page. The opposite of mindless reading is the processing of text by highly effective readers using cognitive strategies. These strategies are described in a fascinating qualitative study that asked expert readers to think aloud regarding what was happening in their minds while they were reading. The lengthy scripts recording these spoken thoughts (i.e., think-alouds) are called *verbal protocols* (Pressley & Afflerbach, 1995). These protocols were categorized and analyzed by researchers to answer specific questions, such as, What is the influence of prior knowledge on expert readers' strategies as they determine the main idea of a text? (Afflerbach, 1990b).

The protocols provide accurate "snapshots" and even "videos" of the ever-changing mental landscape that expert readers construct during reading. Researchers have concluded that reading is "constructively responsive—that is, good readers are always changing their processing in response to the text they are reading" (Pressley & Afflerbach, 1995, p. 2). Instructional Aid 1.1, which follows shortly, defines the seven cognitive strategies of highly effective readers.

According to the research, the most effective way to teach the seven strategies is directly and explicitly. Instructional Aid 1.2 provides a lesson plan template for teaching a cognitive strategy, while Instructional Aid 1.3 contains a sample lesson plan for teaching the summarizing strategy.

RECOMMENDED RESOURCES

McEwan, 2004. *7 Strategies of Highly Effective Readers: Using Cognitive Research to Boost K–8 Achievement.*

Wood, Woloshyn, & Willoughby, 1995. *Cognitive Strategy Instruction for Middle and High Schools.*

RESEARCH ON THE BENEFITS OF TEACHING THE SEVEN STRATEGIES

Dole, 2000; Duffy, 2002.

Instructional Aid 1.1 Seven Strategies of Highly Effective Readers

Strategy	Definition
Activating	"Priming the cognitive pump" in order to recall relevant prior knowledge and experiences from long-term memory in order to extract and construct meaning from text
Inferring	Bringing together what is spoken (written) in the text, what is unspoken (unwritten) in the text, and what is already known by the reader in order to extract and construct meaning from the text
Monitoring-Clarifying	Thinking about how and what one is reading, both during and after the act of reading, for purposes of determining if one is comprehending the text combined with the ability to clarify and fix up any mix-ups
Questioning	Engaging in learning dialogues with text (authors), peers, and teachers through self-questioning, question generation, and question answering
Searching-Selecting	Searching a variety of sources in order to select appropriate information to answer questions, define words and terms, clarify misunderstandings, solve problems, or gather information
Summarizing	Restating the meaning of text in one's own words—different words from those used in the original text
Visualizing-Organizing	Constructing a mental image or graphic organizer for the purpose of extracting and constructing meaning from the text

Instructional Aid 1.2   A Lesson Template for Teaching Cognitive Strategies

Steps	Teacher Script
1. Provide direct instruction regarding the cognitive strategy.	
a. Define and explain the strategy.	
b. Explain the purpose the strategy serves during the act of reading.	
c. Describe the critical attributes of the strategy.	
d. Provide concrete examples and nonexamples of the strategy.	
2. Model the strategy by thinking aloud.	
3. Facilitate guided practice with students.	

Instructional Aid 1.3   A Lesson Plan for Teaching Summarizing

Lesson Template for Teaching Cognitive Strategies	Lesson Plan for Teaching Summarizing
1. Provide direct instruction regarding the cognitive strategy.	
a. Define and explain the strategy.	*Summarizing* is restating in your own words the meaning of what you have read—using different words from those used in the original text—either in written form or a graphic representation (picture or graphic organizer).
b. Explain the purpose the strategy serves during the act of reading.	Summarizing enables a reader to determine what is most important to remember once the reading is completed. Many things we read have only one or two big ideas, and it's important to identify them and restate them for purposes of retention.
c. Describe the critical attributes of the strategy.	A summary has the following characteristics. It • Is short • Is to the point, containing the big idea of the text • Omits trivial information and collapses lists into a word or phrase • Is not a retelling or a "photocopy" of the text

(Continued)

Lesson Template for Teaching Cognitive Strategies	Lesson Plan for Teaching Summarizing
d. Provide concrete examples and nonexamples of the strategy.	Examples of good summaries might include the one-sentence book summaries from *The New York Times* Bestsellers List, an obituary of a famous person, or a report of a basketball or football game that captures the highlights. The mistakes that students commonly make when writing summaries can be more readily avoided by showing students excellent nonexamples (e.g., a paragraph that is too long, has far too many details, or is a complete retelling of the text rather than a statement of the main idea).
2. Model the strategy by thinking aloud.	*Thinking aloud* is a metacognitive activity in which teachers reflect on their behaviors, thoughts, and attitudes regarding what they have read and then speak their thoughts aloud for students. Choose a section of relatively easy text from your discipline and think aloud as you read it, and then also think aloud about how you would go about summarizing it—then do it.
3. Facilitate guided practice with students.	Using easy-to-read content text, read aloud and generate a summary together with the whole class. Using easy-to-read content text, ask students to read with partners and create a summary together. Once students are writing good summaries as partners, assign text and expect students to read it and generate summaries independently.

Engage in Teacher and Student Think-Alouds Daily

I regularly model my own personal problem solving and comprehension of text by verbalizing what is going on in my mind during those processes.

—Kathy Amacher, Middle School Teacher

*T*hinking aloud is a metacognitive activity in which individuals, both teachers and students, reflect on their thinking (i.e., cognitive processing) regarding what they have read and then articulate that thinking for others. When employed by teachers, thinking aloud is one of the most powerful ways to scaffold struggling readers in content classrooms. When employed by students, thinking aloud serves two critical purposes: (1) It increases the comprehension and retention of content, and (2) it serves as an instant assessment of students' comprehension, providing teachers with insights into possible confusion that can be clarified immediately.

When you first introduce thinking aloud to students, you do all of the talking (see Activity 14, Use the I Do It, We Do It, You Do It Lesson Plan). There are two ways to approach thinking aloud for the first time. You can select a portion of your textbook that you believe might be difficult for students to understand and model your own strategy usage *before* you assign it to students. In that case, you would not highlight one specific strategy. Or you can think aloud as part of a lesson designed to teach just one of the strategies. Explain to students what you are doing (thinking aloud) and why (so they can see what's happening in your brain and follow your lead).

Think aloud for students regarding how you make sense of disorganized or "inconsiderate" text, or describe how you make an inference from the text by connecting your personal knowledge and experience with what the author has written. Alternate reading short sections of the chosen text aloud with thinking aloud about how you are mentally processing what you have read. Employ one or more of the seven cognitive strategies of highly effective readers as described earlier in Instructional Aid 1.1, making reflective statements about your thinking, similar to the following:

- **Activating.** *What I just read reminds me of something I learned when I was in high school. I can connect those two things to help me remember the new information.*
- **Inferring.** *I'm sure I know what's going to happen next because the same thing happened to me several years ago.*
- **Monitoring-Clarifying.** *I got confused at this point because I've never seen this word before, so I used the context to figure it out. It helped that I knew a related word in a foreign language.*
- **Questioning.** *I wonder why the author chose this word to describe the Civil War. It seems to me that another word would have made more sense.*
- **Searching-Selecting.** *I had a question when I read this section; I'm either going to ask my friend John who knows a lot about this topic or I'll Google it later.*
- **Summarizing.** *If I jot down key words in the margins during my reading, it helps me to figure out the main idea and write a summary sentence when I finish reading. The word that came to my mind immediately after I finished this sentence was* unjust. *The treatment of the Indians by the explorers in the West doesn't seem fair to me.*
- **Visualizing-Organizing.** *I pictured what was happening here, and it helped me understand how the crime was committed. To help me remember the order in which these events happened, I'm going to construct a timeline in my notes.*

Although skilled readers employ cognitive strategies in a synergistic and interactive way rather than in the step-by-step fashion necessitated by thinking aloud, your students will get the point: There's a lot going on in the brains of skilled readers. They will be fascinated when they hear the multiplicity and variety of your thoughts, and they will soon begin to follow your lead. Your goal is to have all of your students thinking aloud with each other before long.

Some teachers pair up with a colleague, combine their classes, and alternate reading and thinking aloud from the same text to show students that different readers process text in unique ways based on their backgrounds, experience, and strategy usage.

The biggest pitfall for teachers during the initial stages of thinking aloud is slipping out of the metacognitive mode and sliding into the "teaching trap." Be careful not to let these *nonexamples* of thinking aloud creep into your personal think-alouds:

- Explaining what the text means
- Giving a short synopsis of the text
- Teaching what a concept or idea in the text means
- Giving the impression that students should be getting the same meaning from the text as you are
- Lecturing to students about the importance of cognitive strategy usage (save that for another time)
- Giving the impression that you never have any comprehension problems when you read

One way to keep students attentive to your think-aloud is to provide them with a copy of Instructional Aid 1.1. Ask them to highlight the strategies they can identify in your think-aloud and jot down brief notes about what you said. The purpose of thinking aloud is to show students how *you* personally process and respond to what you read. In so doing, you become the "master reader" and your students serve as *cognitive* apprentices. For additional ideas, see also Activity 14, Use the I Do It, We Do It, You Do It Lesson Plan, and Activity 15, Provide Models, Examples, and Nonexamples.

After students have listened to you think aloud during several class periods, build in opportunities for them to think aloud about something they have read. In the beginning, provide easy content-related text. Easy text enables students to understand and practice a cognitive strategy without being cognitively overwhelmed. See Activity 22, Reduce the Cognitive Load, for a discussion of what happens to the brain during cognitive overload and also Activity 24, Use Easy Nonfiction to Build Background Knowledge. If, for example, you find that students are unable to think aloud after you have extensively modeled the process, lower the difficulty level of the text; even the best students can experience this problem.

One instructional approach that focuses students on the text and provides structure for thinking aloud uses sticky flags or arrows to mark the text. For additional ideas, see Activity 3, Teach Students How to Activate Prior Knowledge and Make Connections to New Knowledge, and Activity 12, Teach Students to Mark Text as They Read.

I recommend writing brief scripts for your initial think-alouds. Instructional Aid 2.1 contains a sample script of a social studies teacher think-aloud. Once you have become skilled at thinking aloud, the process will become habitual, and you will no longer be tempted to lecture on the text.

RECOMMENDED RESOURCES

McEwan, 2004. *7 Strategies of Highly Effective Readers: Using Cognitive Research to Boost K–8 Achievement.*
Schoenbach, Greenleaf, Cziko, & Hurwitz, 1999. *Reading for Understanding.*

RESEARCH ON TEACHER MODELING DURING STRATEGY INSTRUCTION

Afflerbach, 2002; Collins, Brown, & Holum, 1991; Duffy, 2002; Pressley, Gaskins, Solic, & Collins, 2005; Trabasso & Bouchard, 2000, 2002.

Instructional Aid 2.1	A Teacher Think-Aloud: A Letter From Thomas Jefferson to Meriwether Lewis (1803)

Read-Aloud Text	Think-Aloud Script
June 20, 1803 To Meriwether Lewis esquire, Captain of the 1st regiment of infantry of the United States of America. Your situation as Secretary of the President of the United States has made you acquainted with the objects of my confidential message of Jan. 18, 1803 to the legislature: you have seen the act they passed, which, tho' expressed in general terms, was meant to sanction those objects, and you are appointed to carry them into execution. Instruments for ascertaining by celestial observations the geography of the country, thro' which you will pass, have been already provided. Light articles for barter, & presents among the Indians, arms for your attendants, say for from 10 to 12 men, boats, tents, & other traveling apparatus, with ammunition, medicine, surgical instruments & provisions you will have prepared with such aids as the Secretary at War can yield in his department; & from him also you will receive authority to engage among our troops, by voluntary agreement, the number of attendants abovementioned, over whom you, as their commanding officer, are invested with all the powers the laws give in such a case. As your movements while within the limits of the US will be better directed by occasional communications, adapted to circumstances as they arise, they will not be noticed here. What follows will respect your proceedings after your departure from the US. Your mission has been communicated to the Ministers here from France, Spain, & Great Britain, and through them to their governments; and such assurances given them as to it's objects, as we trust will satisfy them. The country of Louisiana having been ceded by Spain to France, the passport you have from the Minister of France, the representative of the present sovereign of the country, will be a protection	When I read difficult text or text about an unfamiliar subject, I pay close attention to what I am reading and remain aware of how well I understand it and then clarify or fix up any of my misunderstandings or mix-ups. I'm reading an excerpt of a letter that Thomas Jefferson, the third president of the United States, wrote to Meriwether Lewis, an army officer, who was hired along with Lieutenant William Clark to explore parts of the Louisiana Purchase. I don't know a lot about this topic, but I know that when I am traveling by car west of the Mississippi River, I see quite a few signs about Lewis and Clark. They covered a lot of territory in their travels. As soon as I begin reading, I get a little confused by Jefferson's use of the word "objects." He says that Lewis is well acquainted with the objects of his confidential message. Does he mean the contents or subjects of the message? I'm not sure. Perhaps Jefferson is talking about objectives or goals that Lewis will have for his exploratory mission since he talks about carrying them to execution much as one would set about carrying out a plan. It appears from this text that Lewis is to have whatever he needs to get the job done. Obviously, punctuation and grammar have changed since Thomas Jefferson's day. I notice that rather than using the form "its" to show a possessive, Jefferson uses "it's." I wonder when that usage changed. Jefferson uses the word "communicated" in the first line in the way that we use it today, but then he says that the Missouri River communicates with the Pacific Ocean. Now, he can't mean that the river and the ocean talk to each other. So he must have some other meaning in mind. I'm going to assume (or infer) that he means they just flow into or

(Continued)

Instructional Aid 2.1 (Continued)	
Read-Aloud Text	*Think-Aloud Script*
with all it's subjects: and that from the Minister of England will entitle you to the friendly aid of any traders of that allegiance with whom you may happen to meet. The object of your mission is to explore the Missouri river; & such principal stream of it, as by it's course & communication with the waters of the Pacific ocean, may offer the most direct & practicable water communication across this continent, for the purpose of commerce. Beginning at the mouth of the Missouri, you will take observations of latitude & longitude, at all remarkable points on the river, & especially at the mouths of rivers, at rapids, at islands & other places & objects distinguished by such natural marks & characters of a durable kind, as that they may with certainty be recognized hereafter the courses of the river between these points of observation may be supplied by the compass, the log-line & by time, corrected by the observations themselves. The variations of the compass too, in different places, should be noticed. The interesting points of the portage between the heads of the Missouri & the water offering the best communication with the Pacific ocean, should also be fixed by observation, & the course of that water to the ocean, in the same manner as that of the Missouri.	out of each other, that there's no land interrupting the flow of the water. I ran into another phrase I don't understand—"characters of a durable kind." I know the dictionary meaning of character—someone who plays a role in a play or the kind of person someone is (honest, kind) as in a character trait. But neither of those meanings makes sense in this context. I'm going to reread this to myself again and see if I can make sense of it. I think maybe I get it now. Character in this context seems to be just like the word "characteristic" in our language today. So Jefferson is talking about places along the river with characteristics. I think the word "mark" means landmark here—a place you could identify if you went back again. It seems that Jefferson used the most convoluted ways he could to state something. Language has definitely become more straightforward today.

Teach Students How to Activate Prior Knowledge and Make Connections to New Knowledge

At the root of our ability to learn is our ability to find the experience we have in our memory that is most like the experience we are currently processing.

—Schank (1999, p. 41)

Your goal is to help students acquire meaningful and long-lasting content knowledge. To understand how this happens, an important consideration as you design a lesson, consider your own brain. Think of your long-term memory as a gigantic filing system filled with folders similar to those stored on your computer's hard drive or in an actual filing cabinet in your departmental office. The size of your long-term memory is dictated by how much you know. Amazingly enough, however, its capacity is unlimited.

If you know a lot about a few topics, you have a moderate number of filing cabinets, each stuffed with vast knowledge and experience files. Or you may be someone who knows a lot about a great many subjects. In that case, you have dozens of hanging file drawers, each one filled with multiple cross-references to other drawers. New files are frequently being added to accommodate the additional knowledge you are constructing every day. When you design a new course for your department or take a university class, you undoubtedly have to "buy" a new cabinet. The more files and cabinets your students have, the more readily they can understand and construct new knowledge.

Many struggling readers have very few filing cabinets. They have vast knowledge gaps, exacerbated by their inability to acquire new knowledge through independent reading. Even if they listen attentively to everything you say, without background knowledge or opportunities for previewing important concepts and vocabulary in advance of a lesson (see Activity 16, Preview and Preteach Critical Concepts and Vocabulary), they will have no files ready in which to store new information. Unrelated knowledge and unconnected concepts will rattle around in their short-term and working memories for minutes or even just seconds and then are gone forever.

That is not to say that you will not encounter many struggling readers with excellent listening comprehension and solid background knowledge. You can readily build on that knowledge and improve their comprehension by teaching the seven strategies of highly effective readers (see Activity 1) and providing easy nonfiction based on your content's core concepts (see Activity 24).

The activation of prior knowledge, both before *and* during reading, is a way that readers "prime their cognitive pumps" or turn on their central processing units, so to speak. Whether the knowledge stored in long-term memory is factual, conceptual, or experiential, recalling what is already known about a subject and then connecting it to what is being read greatly increases the likelihood, if not the certainty, that readers will understand and remember what is read while also generating increased levels of motivation and attention. Schank (1999) calls this process *reminding* and explains, "Far from being an irrelevant aspect of memory, reminding is at the heart of how we understand and how we learn" (p. 21).

Activating and retrieving what is known about a specific subject or knowledge domain from the long-term memory system for use in working memory gives readers more information with which to make predictions and generate hypotheses. Activating prior knowledge is not only about asking students what they already know about a specific subject, but it also involves helping them figure out the connections between what they know and what they are reading.

One approach to teaching students how to activate encourages them to make three types of connections as they read a particular piece of text: (1) text to self—connect what is read to personal experiences; (2) text to text—connect what is read to knowledge acquired from reading in other content areas; and (3) text to world—connect what is read to ideas and information acquired from television, movies, magazines, and newspapers (Zimmerman & Keene, 1997).

Some teachers teach students how to use sticky notes on which to make notations relative to the types of connections they are making during their reading. Other teachers prefer that students use sticky flags or arrows, designating different colors of arrows to indicate the different types of connections they are making.

For example, pass out four different colors of sticky arrows to each student along with a piece of easy-to-read content text (one to two arrows of each color depending on the length of the text). Instruct students to place red arrows in the margins of the text where they can make specific connections to something they have personally experienced; green arrows where they can make a specific connection to something they have learned or read in another class; purple arrows where they can make a connection to something they have learned from magazines, newspapers, movies, or television (i.e., popular culture); and blue arrows where the text evokes a strong emotional response (either positive or negative).

Once all students have read the text and placed their arrows appropriately, ask them to pair up and think aloud with each other regarding how the text has activated prior knowledge (i.e., resonated for them). Then ask them to draw conclusions about how this kind of processing can help them understand and then store what they have read in long-term memory.

If you have large numbers of struggling readers in a particular class, consider using one of the oral reading approaches described in Activity 28. You can also readily change the prompts associated with the different colors of arrows if you desire; however, some teachers stick with one set of prompts and colors to avoid confusion.

Remember as you lead students through the process of making connections that there is no substitute for word and world knowledge when it comes to making sense of what one reads. If students don't have basic concepts and prerequisite knowledge, don't be reluctant to fill in the gaps for them *before* they read. See Activity 16, Preview and Preteach Critical Concepts and Vocabulary, and Activity 25, Determine What's Hard for Students and Teach It.

RECOMMENDED RESOURCES

Tovani, 2000. *I Read It, but I Don't Get It: Comprehension Strategies for Adolescent Readers.*

Zimmerman & Keene, 1997. *Mosaic of Thought: Teaching Comprehension in a Reader's Workshop.*

RESEARCH REGARDING THE POWER OF ACTIVATING PRIOR KNOWLEDGE AND MAKING NEW CONNECTIONS

Afflerbach, 1990a, 1990b; Bransford, 1983; Dole, Valencia, Greer, & Wardrop, 1991.

Teach Students How to Infer

A fully explicit text would not only be very long and boring, but it would destroy readers' pleasure in imposing meaning on the text— making it their own.

—Oakhill, Cain, and Yuill (1998, p. 347)

Figuring out what an author has left *unsaid* in the text is often the stated definition of *inferring*. I call it "reading the author's mind." Some call it "reading between the lines." But inferring is actually putting together and reconciling three different sources of information or knowledge: (1) what is written in the text, (2) what is unwritten in the text, and (3) what is already known by the reader in the form of either background knowledge or prior experiences, for the purpose of extracting and constructing meaning from the text.

An inference can pop into readers' minds in several different forms: (1) as a prediction of what might happen later on in the text based on what they have read so far; (2) as a conclusion regarding a concept, proposition, or principle in expository text; or (3) as a brand-new idea formed by combining the readers' prior knowledge with the meaning they have extracted from the text (Anderson & Pearson, 1984).

Inference is defined by van den Broek (1994) as "information that is activated during reading yet not explicitly stated in the text" (p. 556). Many teachers describe inferring to their students as a combination of "reading between the lines" (what is unwritten) and "reading outside the lines" (what is known *only* by the reader). While these phrases are certainly among the most popular definitions of inferring, the expressions are sometimes too figurative to use with struggling readers unless the lesson also includes ample amounts of teacher modeling (thinking aloud) *and* direct explanation. Most students need to "see" the "invisible" writing between the lines that their teachers (or other skilled readers) see in their minds' eyes as they read. They also need to hear what kind of prior knowledge and experiences their teachers and peers are combining with the text to construct meaning.

Inferring is one of the most essential cognitive strategies that skilled readers use. It is frequently employed in combination with other strategies, but its complexity and sophistication, as well as its heavy dependence on background knowledge and vocabulary, often make it a challenge to teach to students. But the task is not impossible if you begin your discussion of inference with examples from students' lives. All students make dozens of inferences every day. They (and we) don't realize how skilled they are at inferential thinking.

To make inferring more relevant to students, develop several scenarios typical to life in middle and high schools. Assign each scenario to a team of three or four student "actors" who will present their improvisations to the class. These two-minutes vignettes will become the "text" from which your students will discover their superb inferential abilities. Here are some scenarios to get you started, but there are no doubt dozens more to be found in the hallways, gymnasiums, and classrooms of your school.

- A jealous girl sees her boyfriend at his locker talking to a girl she has never before seen.
- A student walks into the cafeteria and sees her boyfriend talking to her best friend.
- A large group of girls is trying out for cheerleading, and the sponsors are believed to like one group of girls more than another.
- A student athlete has been told he can only play one sport, and he is torn between choosing baseball or football.
- A student is violating the cell phone rule by text-messaging a friend, asking for what appears to be the answers to a forthcoming quiz.
- A student who is worried about getting into college is overcommitted and has taken on too many responsibilities and obligations, causing a rift with a favorite teacher.

Once you have introduced inferring, you can compare it to the kind of thinking done by detectives or crime scene investigators. Then assign a scenario to each group and give them time to plan and practice their short skit. During the next class period, have each skit performed and then have a debriefing session about the various inferences students made about the actions, motives, and intentions of the improvisational actors. Use the following questions (based on the three types of inferences mentioned earlier) to discuss the scenarios: (1) What do you predict will happen based on the scenario you saw? (2) Is there a moral to this story or any conclusions that can be drawn from it? (3) Did any ideas or questions pop into your mind while you were watching that surprised you? Once you have helped students to make connections between their own experiences and making inferences in reading, you can readily remind them of what an inference is by invoking memories of the skits.

Based on their extensive interviews with expert readers (i.e., the verbal protocols described in Activity 1), Pressley and Afflerbach (1995) identified the following higher-level inferences that skilled readers are constantly making: referents of pronouns (i.e., determining the person to whom a pronoun is referring), meanings of unknown vocabulary, subtle connotations in text, elaborations of ideas based on knowledge of the text or author or subject area, how ideas in a text relate to one's own opinions and theories, the author's purposes in writing the text, the author's assumptions about the world, the author's sources and strategies in writing the text, the text characters' intentions and characteristics, the nature of the world in which the written text takes place, and the conclusions suggested by the text.

While research tells us that inferring is highly dependent on students' background and vocabulary knowledge, most struggling readers *will* become far more inferential when given explicit instruction and modeling regarding what constitutes an inference, whatever the text they are reading.

Another activity to provide students with practice in making inferences can be found in Instructional Aid 4.1, Sample Inference Statements. Use this form to introduce and model the various types of inferences. When I teach inferring to students, I use a PowerPoint presentation with a slide for each of the questions on Aid 4.1. Shortly after students read one of the questions on the screen and I call on someone to answer it, a photo or cartoon appears to validate the answer. In cases where more than one inference can be made, the discussion is vigorous.

Once students have seen examples of inferences (and any nonexamples you care to provide), give them a blank copy of the form (Instructional Aid 4.2) and ask them to write their own inferential statements based on the categories and questions. After students have written their statements, have them share their questions in small groups and come up with their inferences. You may wish to do only a few of these each day and adapt them to content-specific text or objectives.

RECOMMENDED RESOURCE

Kellaher, 2006. *Building Comprehension: Reading Passages With High-Interest Practice Activities.*

This resource is written at a third- and fourth-grade reading level. If you are looking for easy-to-read text to teach the inferring strategy, this inexpensive booklet might be helpful.

RESEARCH TO SUPPORT THE DIRECT TEACHING OF INFERRING

Cain & Oakhill, 1998; Oakhill et al., 1998; van den Broek, 1994.

Instructional Aid 4.1	Sample Inference Statements	
Kind of Inference	**Text Statement**	**Question (Answer)**
Location or setting	The rider hung on tightly with both legs to avoid being tossed to the ground.	Where is this happening? (Rodeo)
Career, occupation, or job	She swirled the frosting around the cake and then placed it in the display case.	What is this person's occupation? (Baker)
Feeling	I won first prize in the science fair.	What is the feeling being described? (Pride, joy, exhilaration, relief, surprise)
Time (clock)	The rooster was crowing.	What time of day is it? (Early in the morning)
Time (season)	Jane was planting seeds in her garden.	What season of the year is it? (The answer depends on where students live. The most likely answer is spring, but in some locales, planting goes on all year long.)
Time (historical period)	The ships were carrying 200,000 soldiers. Not all of the soldiers were English. Some were German. England was paying them to help in the war.	What time in history is it? (Revolutionary War)
Action	He touched every base but was called out at home.	What is the action? (Running the bases after making a hit in a baseball game)
Instrument, tool, or device	"You have a very high fever," she said.	What instrument is being used? (A thermometer)
Cause	My room had never looked so neat.	What is the cause? (I cleaned it; my mother cleaned it; or the cleaning lady cleaned it.)
Effect	I went on the Ferris wheel three times.	What is the effect? (I vomited, I felt nauseous, or I was dizzy.)
Object	There were beanbags, wingbacks, and even a rocking model. I didn't know which one to choose.	What is the object being described? (Chair)
Category	We've been to Disneyland, Sea World, and now we're headed to Legoland.	What is the category? (Theme parks)
Problem	I have to stop eating so many ice-cream cones.	What is the problem? (I've gained weight; my clothes don't fit anymore.)
Solution	I need money to buy a birthday present for Mom.	What is the solution? (Get a job or borrow the money.)

Instructional Aid 4.2 Think-Aloud Form for Making Inferences		
Kind of Inference	*Text Statement*	*Question*
Location or setting		Where is this happening?
Career, occupation, or job		What is this person's occupation?
Feeling		What is the feeling being described?
Time (clock)		What time of day is it?
Time (season)		What season of the year is it?
Time (historical period)		What time in history is it?
Action		What is the action?
Instrument, tool, or device		What instrument is being used?
Cause		What is the cause?
Effect		What is the effect?
Object		What is the object being described?
Category		What is the category?
Problem		What is the problem?
Solution		What is the solution?

Teach Students How to Monitor Their Comprehension

Readers can interpret and evaluate an author's message from the print on the page only to the extent that they possess and call forth the vocabulary, syntactic, rhetorical, topical, analytic, and social knowledge and sensitivities on which the meaning of the text depend.

—Adams (1998, p. 73)

Monitoring is thinking about how and what one is reading, both during and after, for purposes of determining if one actually comprehends the text. Its cognitive partner, *clarifying*, consists of fixing up the mix-ups that interfere with comprehension. Monitoring and clarifying function as a team, so to speak. Monitoring is evaluative; clarifying is regulatory (Baker, 2002). Readers who are monitoring "address text ideas immediately while they are reading . . . [they] try to develop and grapple with ideas, and try to construct meaning" (Beck, McKeown, Hamilton, & Kucan, 1997, p. 6). Clarifying (clearing up confusion) consists of drawing on appropriate fix-up actions based on knowledge (cues) about six different language systems: (1) graphophonic, (2) semantic, (3) pragmatic, (4) syntactic, (5) schematic, and (6) lexical (Collins, Brown, & Newman, 1990).

Highly effective readers fix up their mix-ups in routine and automatic ways, much like skilled drivers adapt to changes in road conditions, detours, or the growing sense that they are lost. *Cues*, in this context, are signals or hints about the way the English language works that are communicated to skilled readers through the printed word. In order to notice those cues, readers have to draw on their background knowledge about language. Consider the variety of cues that children from linguistically rich environments pick up naturally and voracious readers easily learn in school.

For example, as you processed the preceding text, you may have slowed down or even stopped at the word *graphophonic*. You detected a slight mix-up, something that slowed down your reading and raised a question in your mind. *Graphophonic* is a tongue twister of a word, and in order to pronounce it, you likely used your graphophonic knowledge to decode it. Once you "heard" the word in your mind or even said it aloud to practice it, you were able to move on.

At the same time you were decoding *graphophonic*, you were also using *semantic cues* to infer its meaning—having to do with both written language (graph) and spoken words (phon). Without any conscious awareness of doing so, you may have used *pragmatic cues* to enlarge the word's dictionary meaning based on your personal experiences with phonics instruction. You also recognized from the *syntactic cues* that *graphophonic* was an adjective, describing the word *cues*.

Since you already have a well-developed knowledge structure surrounding this word, you drew from *schematic cues* to fit in what you were reading with what you already know. Last, you used *lexical cues* to think of all of the words you know that are related to *graphophonic*—phonics, phonemic, phonological, telephone, phonograph, and so on. And you did all of this processing in a fraction of second.

Struggling readers need to have these cues systematically pointed out to them during your think-alouds of content text. Just as drivers traversing new territory are unable to notice everything around them the first time they drive a route, struggling readers need to read difficult text several times to pick up on cues they may have missed during their first reading. They need to hear skilled readers, like you or other students, noting the cues you've used to monitor and clarify while reading.

In addition to using cues from the various language systems (i.e., the text's linguistic characteristics), highly effective readers also monitor their reading on several other levels by asking and answering questions for themselves. "Self questioners know what they know and, as importantly, know what they don't know" (King, 1989, p. 367).

Here are just a few of the questions that highly effective readers use to monitor and clarify their reading:

1. Does this text satisfy my purpose for reading?

2. Is the text too difficult for me to understand?

3. What is the style of the text?

4. Does the author of the text have any biases?

5. Why am I having such a hard time concentrating on the text?

6. What should I do about the fact that the text is poorly written?

7. Do I have enough background knowledge to understand this text?

8. Where could I find more information to help me?

9. Shall I look up this word I don't know or keep reading?

10. Should I read faster? Or more slowly?

11. Do I need to reread this to increase my understanding?

Use these questions as the basis for thinking aloud and then later give students the questions to answer in pairs as they read and think aloud together.

Teaching students to monitor their own comprehension and clarify their confusion is a day-to-day process that requires consistent modeling and thinking aloud regarding how you personally monitor your own comprehension while reading and exactly how you, fix up your mix-ups while you are reading.

There are several instructional activities you can use to help students practice and become more skilled at monitoring their comprehension and subsequently clarifying their confusion. Use the sticky-arrow approach described in Activity 3, Teach Students How to Activate Prior Knowledge and Make Connections to New Knowledge, but modify it for Monitoring-Clarifying by choosing other colors to signal different types of reading confusion. The prompts might include, (1) If you don't know the meaning of a word, put down a red arrow; (2) if you don't understand what the author is trying to say here, put down a green arrow; (3) if you can't pronounce (identify) this word, put down a purple arrow; and (4) if this section is confusing and poorly written, put down a blue arrow. If you or your students find that keeping track of different colors of arrows and prompts is more confusing than helpful, use one color of arrow and make brief annotations on it. For those students who have a difficult time monitoring their comprehension, this is one possibility to keep them on task and tuned in.

Once confusion sets in, model for students how to use the various approaches found on the Clarifying Tools (Instructional Aid 5.1). Some teachers develop a poster listing these Fix-Up Tools and others prepare a bookmark or laminated card containing the various options.

RECOMMENDED RESOURCES

Meichenbaum & Biemiller, 1998. *Nurturing Independent Learners: Helping Students Take Charge of Their Learning.*
Novak & Gowin, 1984. *Learning How to Learn.*

RESEARCH TO SUPPORT THE IMPORTANCE OF MONITORING-CLARIFYING

Babbs, 1984; Cross & Paris, 1988.

Instructional Aid 5.1 Clarifying Tools

Is there something specific you don't understand—a word, phrase, concept, or idea?

- Ask someone: an adult, an expert, a classmate, the author, or your teacher.

- Look it up: in the dictionary, an encyclopedia, the index, the glossary, on the Internet.

- Make a prediction (inference): "This must be what the author means. I'm going to keep on reading and see if I'm right."

- Predict (infer) the word's meaning based on the context or the word's structure.

Is the text poorly written, disorganized, or very long?

- Chunk it physically: Divide the text into smaller sections and work on one section at one time.

- Chunk it conceptually: Divide the text into big ideas or concepts that fit with the subject or kind of text you're reading.

- Draw a picture, diagram, or graphic organizer.

- Outline it.

Are you confused about the meaning of the text?

- Connect what you have read to your own experience: "This reminds me of the time that…"

- Read the back cover copy, the blurb on the inside front jacket, the preface, a chapter summary, the introduction, a review, or a critique for more clues.

- Read the text again or even twice more, if necessary.

- Stop and think out loud to yourself about what you have read.

- Talk to someone: Think aloud to a friend, family member, or classmate.

- Ignore temporarily the parts you don't understand and keep reading.

Teach Students How to Ask Questions

I keep six honest serving-men
(They taught me all I knew);
Their names are What and Why and When
And How and Where and Who.

—Kipling (1902/1994, p. 69)

The instructional activity I find most helpful for teaching the questioning cognitive strategy (especially teaching students how to ask questions) is an adaptation of the Question-Answer Relationship (QAR) activity originally developed to teach students how to locate answers when they were not readily accessible in the text (Pearson & Johnson, 1978; Raphael, 1984; Raphael & Pearson, 1985; Raphael & Wonnacott, 1985).

This activity, rather than showing students where to look for answers to traditional end-of-chapter questions, focuses on modeling *how to ask specific types of questions,* a far more challenging and productive cognitive assignment. It also facilitates the development of the summarizing and inferring cognitive strategies.

Think aloud and model for students how to ask four types of questions in conjunction with their reading of content text:

1. Questions for which the answer can be found in one place in the text

2. Questions for which students must synthesize information from various parts of the text to come up with an answer

3. Inferential questions for which students must combine what they know with what is stated in the text to find an answer

4. Questions for which students must draw on their own experiences to answer (Raphael, 1984)

After students have been taught the four types of questions using the I Do It, We Do It, You Do It Lesson Plan (Activity 14), have them routinely practice: Expect them to bring questions to class each day from their reading of content text the night before to use in quizzing their classmates. Or ask them to make up questions as they exit from the classroom at the end of a period to be answered by the teacher or fellow students during the next day's class. For a detailed description of this activity and its impact on struggling readers, be sure to consult the recommended resource.

RECOMMENDED RESOURCE

Schoenbach et al., 1999. *Reading for Understanding.*

RESEARCH ON THE POWER OF QUESTIONING

Davey & McBride, 1986; King, 1990; Nolte & Singer, 1985; Raphael, 1984.

Teach Students How to Question the Author

The important thing is not to stop questioning.

—Albert Einstein

Introduce students to the idea of a fallible author or, in the case of text-books, a committee of fallible authors. Explicitly teach and model for students how to

- Identify difficulties with the way the author has presented information or ideas
- Question the author's intent or particular choice of vocabulary
- Zero in on the precise meaning an author is trying to convey
- Recognize when an inference about the author's intentions is needed because the author's conclusions are not clearly articulated

The purpose of questioning the author is to make public the *processes of comprehension.* This questioning ideally takes place immediately following a guided reading session in which the teacher encourages students to grapple with ideas in order to construct meaning. Students can question authors of both narrative and expository texts.

RECOMMENDED RESOURCE

Beck et al., 1997. *Questioning the Author: An Approach for Enhancing Student Engagement With Text.*

Although this book is written for elementary teachers, don't let that discourage you from reading it. Its thesis is a powerful one that all readers need to grasp: Every text has a human fallible author with whom the reader can (and should) interact in a questioning mode.

RESEARCH ON QUESTIONING THE AUTHOR

Underwood & Pearson, 2004.

Teach Students How to Search and Select

[Searching-selecting is] the finding of text, browsing through information, or collecting resources for the purposes of answering questions, solving problems, or gathering information.

—Guthrie and Kirsch (1987, p. 220)

Most educators have the sense that engaging in research or searching on the Internet about subjects currently under study in the classroom is the ideal way to attract distractible but computer-savvy students to the exploration and understanding of new concepts. Educators often assume that students who spend hours surfing the Internet must already know how to search, select, and detect. Consider the possibility, however, that the nonsequential and largely unedited nature of information on the Internet makes it far more challenging to understand than an edited textbook that is limited in scope and written specifically for a well-defined course or student reading level. The number of possible sites or documents that can be retrieved related to a single concept or topic while searching the Internet is overwhelming and may result in cognitive overload (Spires & Estes, 2002), an inappropriate focus on trivial or unrelated information (Harp & Mayer, 1998), or the retrieval of inaccurate information. The editing process in textbook publishing screens out, for the most part, inaccurate, inflammatory, and highly biased text. Navigating the Internet, however, requires a more cautious, if not suspicious, approach to retrieving information.

We cannot expect students to pick up the searching-selecting strategy of text in a specific discipline by osmosis, nor does instruction designed to teach the other six cognitive strategies automatically contribute to the ability of students to search and select (Guthrie & Kirsch, 1987). Students need explicit instruction in how to search for and then select the information they need to accomplish an academic task or a personal information quest. Dreher (2002) suggests a model of locating information that includes the following six steps: (1) Formulate a goal or plan of action, (2) select appropriate categories of a document or text for inspection, (3) extract relevant information from the inspected categories, (4) integrate extracted information with prior knowledge, (5) monitor the completeness of the answer, and (6) recycle through the component processes until the task is complete (p. 295). Regularly model your thinking regarding how you formulate a search question, find possible answers, and select the most logical one for your question.

Searching and selecting is a little like prospecting for gold—looking for nuggets of information and determining whether they are real or fool's gold. I use the following set of prompts to teach searching and selecting using this mining metaphor:

- *Reflect*. Determine what you are looking for and decide where to look.
- *Prospect*. Dig on the Internet to identify prospective sources.
- *Detect*. Review the books, Web sites, periodicals, and other resources you have found to determine which ones will give you what you need.
- *Select*. Pick out what is most important in the sources you have found.
- *Connect*. Put together what you have found to answer your questions.

These steps can be found in Instructional Aid 8.1, How to Search and Select: A Poster.

RECOMMENDED RESOURCES

Dreher, M. J. (1993). "Reading to Locate Information: Societal and Educational Perspectives." *Contemporary Educational Psychology.*
Dreher, M. J., & Guthrie, J. T. (1990). "Cognitive Processes in Textbook Search Tasks." *Reading Research Quarterly.*

RESEARCH SHOWING THE IMPORTANCE OF SEARCHING AND SELECTING

Guthrie & Kirsch, 1987.

Instructional Aid 8.1	How to Search and Select: A Poster

How to Search and Select

Reflect: Determine what you are looking for and decide where to look.

Prospect: Go digging in library catalogs and on the Internet to identify prospective sources.

Detect: Review the books, Web sites, periodicals, and other resources you have found to determine which ones will give you what you need.

Select: Pick out what is most important in the sources you have found.

Connect: Put together what you have found to answer your questions.

Teach Students How to Summarize

[In writing a summary], if you find yourself sticking to the original language and making only minor changes to the wording, then you probably don't understand [what you have read].

—University of Washington Psychology
Writing Center (2006, p. 2)

You can never do too much modeling and practicing of summarizing for and with students. It is one of the most important cognitive strategies in terms of academic success, and it requires mindful and skilled reading. Recall the sample lesson for teaching summarizing found in Instructional Aid 1.3.

There are numerous instructional activities to facilitate the development of summarizing, but in the end, as noted in the foregoing quotation, summarizing is dependent on the reader's comprehension of the text. If students don't get it, they can't summarize it. Encourage and model for students how to dig for meaning, ask questions, interrogate the author, and diligently consult teachers in afterschool homework sessions.

Hang this motto on your classroom wall: "Read four. Learn more." It reminds students that it's not enough to read it once and give up. Skilled readers keep at it until they get it. Put up a poster containing this Walt Whitman quote (from Gilbar, 1990):

The process of reading is not a half-sleep, but in the highest sense, an exercise, a gymnast's struggle; that the reader is to do something

37

for himself [herself], must be on the alert, must himself [herself] construct indeed the poem, argument, history, metaphysical essay—the text furnishing the hints, the clue, the start or framework.

When you first introduce the summarizing strategy, keep your modeling simple and the text samples easy. Think aloud while summarizing what has been learned in a class period by choosing a key word and writing a sentence or drawing a picture. Model writing a summary of a short section of the textbook. After you have modeled the process several times for students during two or three class periods, then move on to writing a summary together with the whole class. When you are satisfied that everyone is beginning to understand the process, then pair students to come up with key words and write sentences together.

Only after struggling readers have seen you model summarizing, participated in a guided practice with the whole class together, and had multiple opportunities to work with partners to choose key words and write summarizing sentences should you move on to a more complex summarizing model: the Five C's of Summarizing. The five C's are *comprehend, chunk, compact, conceptualize,* and *connect.* See Instructional Aids 9.1 through 9.5 for definitions and graphic organizers for each of the C's.

The Five C's of Summarizing, when taught using the I Do It, We Do It Lesson Plan (Activity 14), give students a systematic way to approach the summarizing of a long article, a full-length book, or a chapter in the textbook. Teachers in my workshops use the approach to summarize research studies for graduate classes. Model and teach just one C at a time, thinking aloud and providing multiple examples and nonexamples over several days or a week. Choose easy content text. Once each C has been modeled, taught, and practiced several times, students can use all five C's in combination to complete independent summarizing tasks.

RECOMMENDED RESOURCE

Saphier & Haley, 1993b. *Summarizers: Activity Structures to Support Integration and Retention of New Learning.*

RESEARCH ON THE POWER OF SUMMARIZATION

Afflerbach & Johnston, 1984; Armbruster, Anderson, & Ostertag, 1987; Bean & Steenwyk, 1984; Brown & Day, 1983.

Instructional Aid 9.1   The Five C's of Summarizing: Comprehend

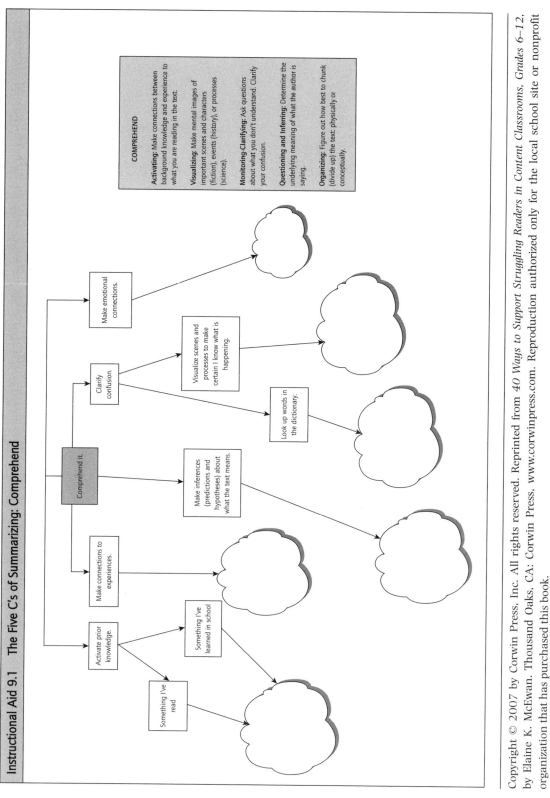

COMPREHEND

Activating: Make connections between background knowledge and experience to what you are reading in the text.

Visualizing: Make mental images of important scenes and characters (fiction), events (history), or processes (science).

Monitoring-Clarifying: Ask questions about what you don't understand. Clarify your confusion.

Questioning and Inferring: Determine the underlying meaning of what the author is saying.

Organizing: Figure out how best to chunk (divide up) the text: physically or conceptually.

Comprehend it.

Activate prior knowledge.

Make connections to experiences.

Make emotional connections.

Clarify confusion.

Something I've read

Something I've learned in school

Make inferences (predictions and hypotheses) about what the text means.

Visualize scenes and processes to make certain I know what is happening.

Look up words in the dictionary.

Instructional Aid 9.2   The Five C's of Summarizing: Chunk

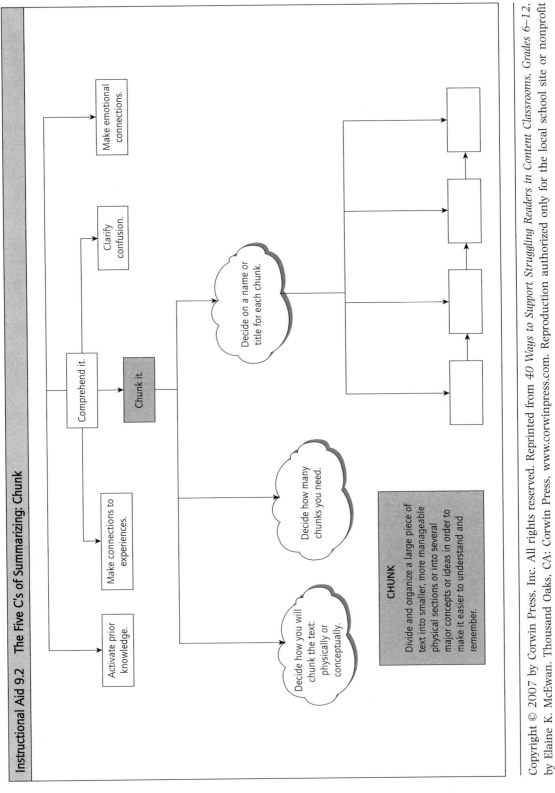

Instructional Aid 9.3   The Five C's of Summarizing: Compact

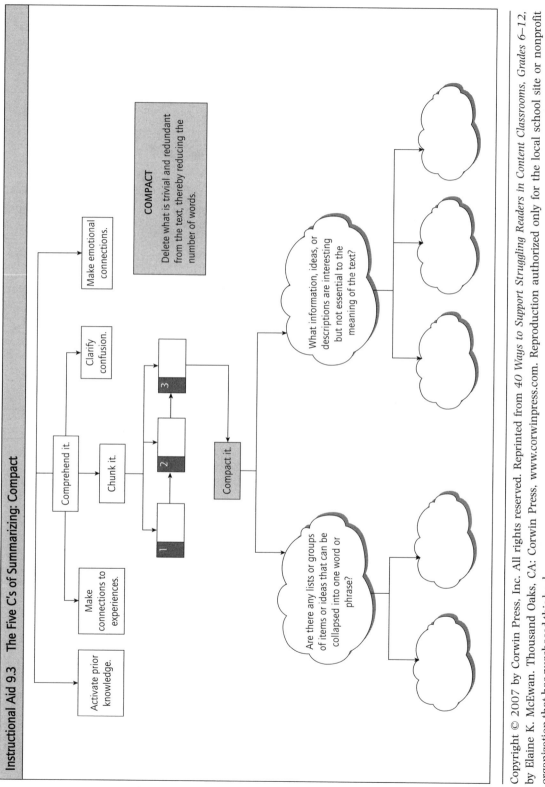

Instructional Aid 9.4   The Five C's of Summarizing: Conceptualize

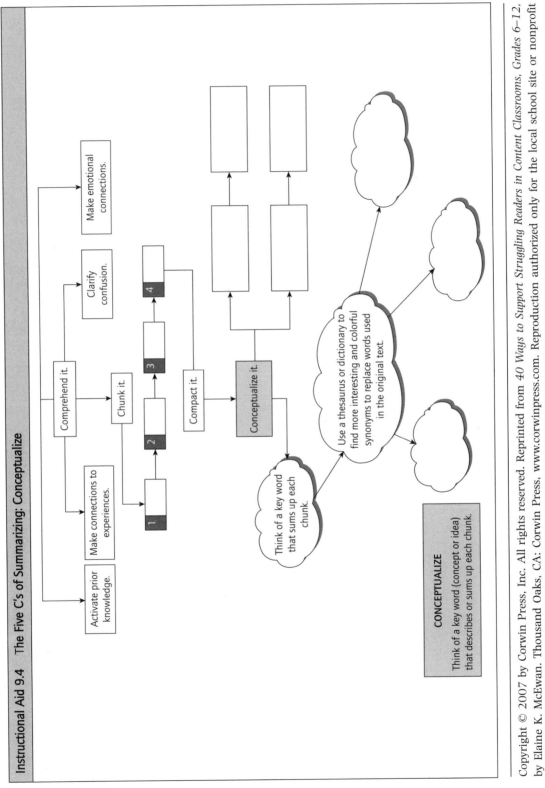

CONCEPTUALIZE

Think of a key word (concept or idea)
that describes or sums up each chunk.

Instructional Aid 9.5 The Five C's of Summarizing: Connect

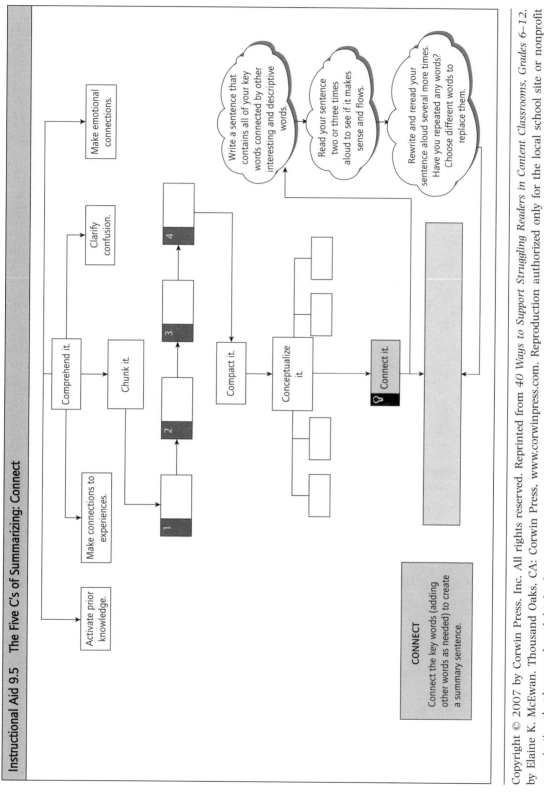

CONNECT

Connect the key words (adding other words as needed) to create a summary sentence.

Activate prior knowledge.

Make connections to experiences.

Comprehend it.

Clarify confusion.

Make emotional connections.

Chunk it.

Compact it.

Conceptualize it.

Connect it.

Write a sentence that contains all of your key words connected by other interesting and descriptive words.

Read your sentence two or three times aloud to see if it makes sense and flows.

Rewrite and reread your sentence aloud several more times. Have you repeated any words? Choose different words to replace them.

Teach Students How to Graphically Organize Text and Concepts by Chunking

Any sort of systematic attention to clues that reveal how authors attempt to relate ideas to one another or any sort of systematic attempt to impose structure upon a text, especially in some sort of visual representation of the relationships among key ideas, facilitates comprehension as well as both short-term and long-term memory for the text.

—Pearson and Fielding (1991, p. 832)

One of the major challenges for struggling readers is overcoming the dread they feel when faced with a long, difficult reading assignment. One way to help your students grapple with this challenge is by teaching them how to graphically chunk text.

Sometimes the term *chunk* means to physically split up a long reading selection into shorter sections of text, stopping after each section to make notes in the margin. In this section, chunking refers to organizing text into smaller conceptual units in order to figure out its gist or main idea. Conceptual chunking aims to bring a sense of organization and structure to a topic or concept, making it easier to comprehend, summarize, and remember.

Research is clear about the importance of learners approaching text or new material with some preconceived organizational structure in mind. Here are some specifics mentioned by Bransford, Brown, and Cocking (2000). The italics in these bulleted points have been added.

- Effective comprehension and thinking require a coherent understanding of the *organizing* principles in any subject matter; understanding the essential features of the problems of various school subjects will lead to better reasoning and problem solving. (See Activity 23, Teach the Structure of Your Discipline.)
- Transfer and wide application of learning are most likely to occur when learners achieve an *organized* and coherent understanding of the material.
- Learning and understanding can be facilitated by emphasizing *organized*, coherent bodies of knowledge (in which specific facts and details are embedded).
- In-depth understanding requires detailed knowledge of the facts within a domain. The key attribute of expertise is a detailed and *organized* understanding of the important facts within a specific domain. (pp. 238–239)

When I am explaining to teachers how to chunk text or ideas conceptually, we begin with something familiar—their lives. I first tell them how I chunk my own life using geographical locations—(1) Michigan, (2) Illinois, and (3) Arizona—and share my key words: cold, colder, and comfortable. I then ask them to divide (chunk) their lives into three to five sections, title each section with a key word, write a short sentence using the key word, and then connect the sentences together into a short autobiography.

I have discovered that there are as many ways to chunk a life as there are participants in a workshop: time periods, places where people have lived, ideas or philosophies they have espoused during different periods, cars they have driven, schools they have attended, or types of roles and relationships they have experienced. For this kind of chunking, the graphic organizer that works best is a timeline.

If you have reviewed the Five C's of Summarizing as described in Activity 9, Teach Students How to Summarize, you will immediately recognize the C's in the following instructional activity. Most individuals are able to quickly comprehend their lives. After all, they have lived them and know them as well as anyone could. However, making a decision as to how to chunk their lives usually takes some thinking. There are many possibilities for every individual and there is no right way to chunk a life—or a piece of content text.

However, once the conceptual chunking (organizing) has been done, participants can readily determine what details of their lives are irrelevant to their summaries. They can quickly choose key words and then use those key words to write sentences. The goal of using the Five C's of Summarizing is to help readers process and retain the big ideas of the text, not create a boilerplate summary that is identical to everyone else's. Of course, if you expect students to extract precise meanings from the text, you will undoubtedly be more prescriptive in your instructions and expectations. In that case, giving students an advance summary of the most important ideas and encouraging them to find support for your statements may be a more beneficial use of their time.

In the foregoing chunking activity, we decided how to chunk our lives in order to write a short autobiography. That was familiar territory for everyone. But chunking content text requires a deeper understanding of the possible ways one might organize text or concepts in the various disciplines. See also Activity 23, Teach the Structure of Your Discipline.

For example, social studies text can be chunked conceptually in the following ways:

- By topics, ideas, or categories (e.g., The Causes of the Civil War, Battles of the Civil War, and How the Civil War Ended)
- By time periods (e.g., The Middle Ages, The Renaissance, Discovery and Reformation, and The Enlightenment)
- By philosophies or beliefs (e.g., Judaism, Christianity, Islam, and Buddhism)
- By noted historical figures (e.g., Thomas Jefferson, Meriwether Lewis, and William Clark)
- By geographical regions (e.g., Southwestern U.S., Northwestern U.S., and Midwestern U.S.)
- By culture-language-ethnic groups (e.g., Lakota, Nakota, and Dakota)
- By comparing and contrasting two or more concepts, philosophies, places, or people
- By determining cause-and-effect relationships

Science text (expository) and concepts can be chunked conceptually in these ways:

- By life cycles phases (e.g., egg, caterpillar, chrysalis, and butterfly)
- By steps in a process (e.g., light-dependent reactions and light-independent reactions)
- By time periods (e.g., eras, periods, and epochs)

- By chemical reactions (e.g., $6\ H_2O + 6\ CO_2 = C_6H_{12}O_6 + 6\ O_2$)
- By properties (e.g., igneous rocks, sedimentary rocks, and meta-morphic rocks)
- By determining cause-and-effect relationships

Fiction text (narrative) can be chunked conceptually in the following ways:

- By characters
- By story scenes
- By story elements or grammar
- By determining cause-and-effect relationships
- By comparing and contrasting characters, settings, plots, and so forth

One of the most powerful ways that readers can organize and visually display the various chunks they find in their reading is by constructing graphic organizers. For example, periods of history or scientific eras are best organized in timelines. The effects of various shifts in foreign policy and diplomacy are best displayed in a cause-and-effect organizer. Science processes lend themselves well to flow charts. Character analysis in fiction can be graphically presented in a character map or web.

Average and above-average students may well have mastered the skills needed to graphically organize large amounts of text or multiple complex topics, but struggling readers need to see teachers model the construction of organizers as well as examples and nonexamples of various types of organizers that are relevant to specific content areas. Instructional Aid 10.1 contains a listing of graphic organizers grouped by their applicability to certain disciplines and types of text.

RECOMMENDED REOSOURCES

Hyerle, 2004. *Student Successes With Thinking Maps®: School-Based Research, Results, and Models for Achievement Using Visual Tools.*

Jones, Pierce, & Hunter, 1988. "Teaching Students to Construct Graphic Representations." *Educational Leadership.*

RESEARCH ON THE POWER OF GRAPHICALLY ORGANIZING

Armbruster, Anderson, & Meyer, 1991; Borduin, Borduin, & Manley, 1994; Sinatra, Stahl-Gemake, & Berg, 1984.

Instructional Aid 10.1	Graphic Organizers for Content Instruction	
Organizers for Nonfiction (Expository Text)	*Organizers for Fiction (Narrative Text)*	*Organizers for Mathematics*
Analogy organizer	Concept map	Chart
Cause-effect	Matrix	Concept map
Chain of command	Network tree	Diagram
Chain of events	Picture	Equation
Chart	Problem-solution outline	Image
Compare-contrast matrix	Puzzle	Matrix
Concept map	Relay summary	Picture
Concept wheel	Semantic features analysis	Semantic features analysis
Continuum	Semantic word map	Semantic word map
Crossword puzzle	Spider map	
Cycle	Story frame	
Diagram	Story grammar	
Entailment mesh	Story map	
Fishbone diagram	Talking drawings	
Flow chart	Timeline	
Frayer model	Venn diagram	
Grid	Web	
Hierarchy	Why-because pursuit chart	
Historical figure character map		
Human interaction outline		
List		
Semantic features analysis		
Semantic word map		

11

Use and Teach Concept Maps

Highly meaningful learning that includes novel problem solving and creativity is only possible in domains of knowledge where the learner has considerable, well-organized prior knowledge.

—Novak (1998, p. 24)

Graphic organizers are very popular and when constructed by students during independent reading, they are highly effective in helping them to make sense of challenging or poorly organized text. Less understood and appreciated for its power to help struggling readers to more easily construct long-lasting knowledge is the concept map: a graphic representation that identifies key concepts and joins them with connecting words showing the nature of their relationships.

Concept maps differ from traditional graphic organizers in that they require students to specify precisely how concepts are related to one another. Concept maps are excellent tools for helping you to organize the knowledge of your discipline for instruction as well as for assisting struggling readers to find the key concepts and principles in lectures, readings, and discussions.

Constructing concept maps helps to build a deep understanding of the relationships between concepts, increases the ability to choose meaningful connecting words, and develops an understanding of the directionality of the relationships.

Concept maps can be used in the following ways: (1) to take notes during lectures or listening; (2) to guide reading assignments; (3) as a study guide for test preparation; (4) as a tool to assist in writing a summary of the text; or (5) as an ongoing summarizing and review of the concepts discussed during each class period.

If you are intrigued by the possibility of using concept maps in your classroom, consult the recommended resource for how to begin. Some teachers begin each new unit or textbook chapter with a giant concept map posted on the wall and fill in the blanks together with their students. This omnipresent instructional aid is especially valuable to struggling readers who, although they may be overwhelmed by a 50-page chapter of text, can readily grasp the concepts and their relationships in a simple organizer. Use easy-reading nonfiction text when you teach your students how to construct concept maps. For example, Instructional Aid 11.1 displays a concept map based on an easy book about dinosaurs. Once students have grasped the idea of the concept map by working with easy text, they will be more confident in working with difficult content.

RECOMMENDED RESOURCE

Novak, 1998. *Learning, Creating, and Using Knowledge: Concept Maps as Facilitative Tools in Schools and Corporations.*

RESEARCH ON THE POWER OF CONSTRUCTING CONCEPT MAPS

Jonassen, Beissner, & Yacci, 1993; Novak & Gowin, 1984; Wandersee, 1990.

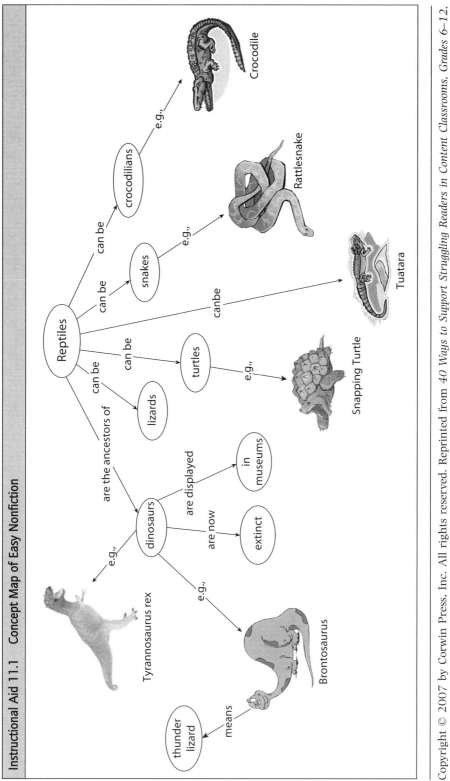

Instructional Aid 11.1   Concept Map of Easy Nonfiction

Reptiles

can be → crocodilians → e.g., → Crocodile

can be → snakes → e.g., → Rattlesnake

canbe → Tuatara

can be → turtles → e.g., → Snapping Turtle

can be → lizards

are the ancestors of → dinosaurs

dinosaurs → are displayed → in museums

dinosaurs → are now → extinct

dinosaurs → e.g., → Tyrannosaurus rex

dinosaurs → e.g., → Brontosaurus

Brontosaurus → means → thunder lizard

Teach Students How to Mark Text as They Read

Mindless reading is the literary equivalent of driving for miles without remembering how you got there.

—Feller (2006, p. 1)

Reading text that is badly written is a challenge, even for the best readers. Struggling readers, however, are at an even greater disadvantage. They often lack background knowledge and vocabulary and are unable to make meaningful connections between the text and anything they know or have experienced. Students who are engaged in the physical act of marking text while reading (i.e., making notations in the margins, highlighting the most important idea, writing a question on a sticky note, or placing a brightly colored sticky arrow or flag on a word they don't know) are more likely to stay focused on text, cognitively process it, and retain what they have read.

I call the physical objects that help readers stay focused on the printed page *props* (e.g., a template on which to take notes, prompts to which they must respond, highlighters in different colors, or sticky notes or arrows). My favorite reading props are sticky arrows. I have two small leather cases to hold my arrows, one for my purse and one on my desktop. Since the advent of these helpful reading props, I've tossed out the highlighters that I previously used. Sticky arrows enable me to mark places in my reading that I want to remember: a word or phrase I want to look up in the dictionary or Google, places in the text where I am confused and need to come back and reread if reading further in the text doesn't clarify my confusion, or a place that contains an idea that will be important to include in my summary. This technique is especially helpful when I am reading books that I have borrowed from the library or a friend. And I can usually reclaim the arrows and reuse them, once I have finished my reading.

Sticky arrows have no magical powers to increase comprehension, but they do help me to stay focused on the text—an important prerequisite to comprehension. When I put down an arrow, I am more likely to interact with and process the text. Some teachers create their own custom sticky flags containing prompts that specifically relate to their content. See Instructional Aid 12.1, a set of math stickies created by middle school math teacher Kim Buck. I recommend Easy-Stick Double Stick Adhesive (Removable Bond) for creating your own sticky flags. Give each student a block of sticky flags containing one of each kind, run a strip of the adhesive on the reverse side of the block and ask students to cut them up into strips. The "sticky stuff" will last through two or three readings if the sticky flags are handled carefully. Office supply stores carry the product. Call 1-800-321-0253 for further information.

RECOMMENDED RESOURCE

Harvey & Goudvis, 2000. *Strategies That Work: Teaching Comprehension to Increase Understanding.*

RESEARCH TO SUPPORT THE IMPORTANCE OF ATTENDING TO TEXT WHILE READING

Schooler et al., 2004.

Instructional Aid 12.1 Master for Math Stickies

I know this well enough to explain it to someone else.	I know this well enough to explain it to someone else.	I know this well enough to explain it to someone else.
This connects to something I know or have done.	This connects to something I know or have done.	This connects to something I know or have done.
I need multiplication facts to work this problem.	I need multiplication facts to work this problem.	I need multiplication facts to work this problem.
I need to put this in my math notebook.	I need to put this in my math notebook.	I need to put this in my math notebook.
I have a bright idea about how to use this.	I have a bright idea about how to use this.	I have a bright idea about how to use this.
I don't understand it.	I don't understand it.	I don't understand it.

SOURCE: Used with permission of Kim Buck.

Reproduction of material from this book is authorized only for the local school site or nonprofit organization that has purchased *40 Ways to Support Struggling Readers in Content Classrooms, Grades 6–12*, by Elaine K. McEwan. Thousand Oaks, CA: Corwin Press, www.corwinpress.com.

Provide Advance Organizers Before Lessons

To say that you have taught when students haven't learned is to say you have sold when no one has bought.

—Madeline Hunter, 1989 Presentation,
Carol Stream, Illinois

An advance man (or woman) is someone who travels ahead of the main attraction and stirs up interest and promotes attendance. In the olden days, an advance man arrived before the circus to put up posters all over town and create a sense of anticipation and desire among the younger set. Today, advance men and women arrive before the politicians show up to ensure enthusiastic crowds of supporters.

Psychologist David Ausubel (1960) coined the phrase *advance organizer* to describe the ways teachers can help students activate prior knowledge and experience, connect it to new learning, and then retain concepts and information from classroom presentations. The contemporary term for helping students activate prior knowledge or giving them important knowledge ahead of the lesson is called *front-loading*. Advance organizers can be simple statements like these:

- Let me explain what we are going to do today and why.
- We are learning this because . . .

- Let me show you how what we have learned today connects to what we did yesterday.
- When you learn how to . . . you will be able to . . . (Meichenbaum & Biemiller, 1998, p. 119)

Advance organizers can be brief activities, dazzling demonstrations, compelling questions, or visual organizers, such as concept maps that engage students in the lesson to come. In addition to being both visual and verbal, advance organizers can also be metaphorical in nature. For example, in discussing the importance of cognitive processing with students, I use a computer analogy, comparing their brains to the central processing unit (CPU) of a computer and challenging them to "turn on their CPUs" before they tackle a reading or writing assignment.

Madeline Hunter (2004) called this part of the lesson the *anticipatory set* but cautioned against using an elephant to teach the color gray. The purpose of an advance organizer is to help students activate knowledge and experiences in their long-term memories, retrieve what they have stored, and then subsequently connect it to the new information on the agenda, not to be the main attraction of the lesson.

As tempting as it may be to skip the advance organizer, counting on the objective you have copied from the standards to serve the purpose, remember that only the most motivated students will be able to make the cognitive leap from the words on the board to the point of your lesson. Struggling readers are totally dependent on the teacher for help in activating. They also need help in figuring out the rationale for the lesson. What's the point in paying attention?

If you're about to launch into a lesson on how to write a paragraph in response to reading science text, take a minute to quiz students regarding the relevance to their lives of engaging in this activity. Ask students, "Why do you think it would be important for you to be able to read and process science information?" Here are some answers you might get: One student has a family member with a rare form of cancer that requires specialized treatments. He wants to be able to read a description of the condition and possible treatment options on the Internet in order to help his parents. Another student thinks she might like to work in a medical profession in the future. Being able to read and comprehend science text is essential for pursuing that kind of career. Another student wants to join the Marines and needs to do well on the high school high-stakes test. Even though he doesn't like science, he needs to do well to get to the next step. A discussion like this won't take long, but it could be just what you need to persuade struggling readers to partner with you in trying to make sense of a complicated subject.

Consider your learning objective as well as the needs of your students and then develop an advance organizer to initiate the following cognitive processes: (1) retrieve prior knowledge and experience from long-term memory, (2) connect it to the new information or skills on the agenda for the day, (3) process it in working memory to create new learning, and (4) send the "bundle" to long-term memory for retrieval the following day.

Helping students to activate (get their brains up and moving for the day) is the biggest challenge of teaching, especially if you work with students who lack basic concepts or are struggling to learn a second language. Although writing a state standard on the board before each lesson may satisfy an observing administrator, it won't do a thing for struggling readers. Unless you can discover *something* that your students already know or have experienced to provide that essential bridge to meaningful learning, your beautifully prepared lesson will be ineffective. As a teacher, you must not only be the main act, but also the advance man (or woman).

RECOMMENDED RESOURCES

Meichenbaum & Biemiller, 1998. *Nurturing Independent Learners: Helping Students Take Charge of Their Learning.*
Novak & Gowin, 1984. *Learning How to Learn.*

RESEARCH SHOWING THE IMPORTANCE OF LEARNERS MAKING CONNECTIONS

Ausubel, 1960, 1978; Ausubel, Novak, & Hanesian, 1978.

Use the I Do It, We Do It, You Do It Lesson Plan

Whenever I have a class that needs to develop note-taking skills, I model for students on the overhead or whiteboard precisely what they should be writing down in their notebooks as a result of something I have said. In the beginning weeks of the school year I am more deliberate about writing notes out for them, and as the year goes by I am able to just "speak" notes to them to get them to listen and take notes without relying on the overhead or whiteboard. I always collect students' notebooks to see whether they are getting the critical ideas from both my lectures and our discussions.

—Rose Bender, High School History Teacher

The I Do It, We Do It, You Do It Lesson Plan is an ideal way to support struggling readers. With this approach, students will be able to understand and master what your lesson was designed to teach. And they will be able to complete the homework assignment independently. This approach stands in stark contrast to the typical agenda in some content classes:

- Teacher talks, lectures, and explains new material.
- With five minutes remaining in the class, teacher gives homework assignment to students (e.g., complete this graphic organizer, write a short summary, write a letter to your senator about your opinion on this issue).
- The bell rings.

If you are serious about expecting all students to complete assignments proficiently, provide well-executed models for students to inspect and provide further support by doing a sample together with the entire class. Once you have completed these steps, then guide pairs of students in additional practice as necessary. Do all of this *before* you expect students to complete an assignment independently. Not only will the quality of students' work improve, but their understanding and retention of content will also increase.

Using this lesson plan requires that we pay constant attention to our students' work products as a means of assessing our teaching effectiveness. Our natural inclination as teachers is to skip the We Do It step because we feel pressured by time and curricular constraints. We move forward, however, at the risk of losing our struggling students. I recently discovered that I had been fast-forwarding through this step in a workshop, almost without thinking, thereby depriving my students of achieving mastery of the assigned task—the writing of a script to use in dealing with a difficult colleague. I modeled the process for them several times and then assumed that they were ready to work independently on developing their own personal scripts. I wasn't happy with the results I was getting. Some participants weren't completing their scripts even though there was plenty of time. Others found more pressing tasks to take care of (e.g., checking e-mail, making a cell phone call, or taking a trip to the coffee table). There is always the tendency to blame students (participants) at this point. They aren't motivated. They don't care. However, the minute I inserted the We Do It step back into the lesson, there was success for all. We did each step of the script together as a whole group, one prompt at a time, answering questions and hearing sample statements from individuals as we went. The result: Every participant enthusiastically completed the assignment. The quality of the work products and hence the level of student learning increased dramatically. If competent professional teachers and administrators need the We Do It part of the lesson plan to complete an assignment, struggling readers need it (and other students as well).

Instructional Aid 14.1 shows the steps in the I Do It lesson plan. See also the following approaches for additional help with developing an I Do It lesson: Activity 2, Engage in Teacher and Student Think-Alouds Daily, and Activity 15, Provide Models, Examples, and Nonexamples.

RECOMMENDED RESOURCE

Hunter, 2004. *Madeline Hunter's Mastery Teaching: Increasing Instructional Effectiveness in Elementary and Secondary Schools.*

RECOMMENDED RESEARCH IN SUPPORT OF DIRECT AND EXPLICIT INSTRUCTION FOR STRUGGLING READERS

Duffy, 2002; Gaskins, Laird, O'Hara, Scott, & Cress, 2002.

Instructional Aid 14.1   I Do It, We Do It, You Do It Lesson Plan Form

Step	Description	Teacher Script
Anticipatory Set	Teacher activates background knowledge and experiences of students in order to build connections to the lesson objective.	
I Do, You Watch	Teacher models how to do what the students will be expected to do as an outcome of the lesson.	
I Do, You Help	Teacher models once again with the help of selected students.	
We Do, I Help	All students complete some part of the task under the guidance of the teacher, preferably in partners.	
You Do, I Watch	All students complete the task independently while still under the teacher's supervision.	
Closure, Summarizing Statement	Teacher summarizes the purpose and possible applications of the task and gives a homework assignment if applicable.	

SOURCE: Adapted from Shannon Coombs' Modeling Lesson Design based on the work of Madeline Hunter and developed by the staff of the Douglas County (NV) School District.

Reproduction of material from this book is authorized only for the local school site or nonprofit organization that has purchased *40 Ways to Support Struggling Readers in Content Classrooms, Grades 6–12,* by Elaine K. McEwan. Thousand Oaks, CA: Corwin Press. www.corwinpress.com.

Provide Models, Examples, and Nonexamples

We do not teach our children wisely and well if certain keystone stances are not topmost in our minds and hearts. Modeling is one of those keystone precepts. The only thing worse than faulty modeling is a teacher who does not credit the power of modeling.

—Pickard (2005, p. 35)

If your students don't understand or retain what you are teaching them, use the cognitive apprenticeship model as a powerful way to accelerate learning for all students (Collins et al., 1990; Collins et al., 1991). In a traditional apprenticeship (e.g., one in the trades such as plumbing or carpentry), the expert tradesperson shows the apprentice how to do a task and then gradually gives over more and more of the responsibility for the task to the apprentice. In a cognitive apprenticeship, it is the teacher's thinking and problem solving that are made visible to students through modeling. Regrettably, teacher modeling is rarely seen in many classrooms.

In a study of the frequency of general education teachers' classroom behaviors, modeling and role-playing were among the lowest. Modeling was observed less than 5% of the time and role-playing hardly ever. At the other end of the frequency continuum, lecturing was observed slightly more than half the time while giving directions occurred nearly a quarter of the time (Schumaker et al., 2002).

Modeling can take several forms in your classroom:

- Thinking aloud regarding your cognitive processing of text (e.g., sharing with students how you make connections between what you know and something that you've read in the text or how you figured out what the author was inferring). For further assistance with thinking aloud, see Activity 2, Engage in Teacher and Student Think-Alouds Daily.
- Demonstrating or showing your students explicitly how you would complete an assignment (e.g., writing a summary of an article, taking notes, constructing a graphic organizer, or giving a speech)
- Showing first-rate completed examples of a work product (e.g., a summary paragraph or graphic organizer) as well as substandard nonexamples that help students differentiate between a good one and an unacceptable one
- Showing students how to work a math problem, set up an experiment, or follow a specific safety procedure in the laboratory
- Acting out, role-playing, or developing simulations. See Instructional Aid 15.1, A Simulation for Mitosis (or Meiosis).
- Explaining, telling, and giving directions *are* essential teaching moves, but unless they are accompanied by various types of modeling, the likelihood of struggling readers achieving success is small. Never assume that because students have spent years in school, they have been explicitly taught or have somehow figured out on their own how to do what you want them to do. For further information on a variety of essential teaching moves, see Activity 29, Vary Your Models, Moves, and Activities.

RECOMMENDED RESOURCES

Collins et al., 1991. "Cognitive Apprenticeship: Making Thinking Visible." *American Educator.*
Rose, 1995. "Apprenticeship and Exploration: A New Approach to Literacy Instruction." *Scholastic Literacy Research.*

RESEARCH SUPPORTING THE IMPORTANCE OF MODELING FOR STUDENTS

Collins et al., 1990; Collins et al., 1991.

Instructional Aid 15.1 A Simulation for Mitosis (or Meiosis)

Stepping Into Cell Division

1. Each student gets two pieces of paper and a pencil or pen.

2. Each student places his or her papers horizontally on the floor, one page in front of each foot (works best on tile floors).

3. Students stand on the inside half of each sheet—one foot per paper—and then trace their feet (it's no problem if feet extend beyond the paper; just have students trace the part of their foot that is on the paper). Each drawn foot represents an unduplicated chromosome. Each pair of feet represents a homologous pair of unduplicated chromosomes.

4. Explain to students our classroom is a cell that is in the G1 stage of Interphase, a period of rapid cell growth. Count the number of chromosomes in your cell (it should be twice your number of students).

5. Tell students that as cells continue to grow, they reach a point where they must divide again. To prepare for this, cells must copy their chromosomes. Show this replication (S phase of Interphase) by having the students move their feet to the outside half of each paper and trace again. Now each piece of paper represents a duplicated chromosome (with two sister chromatids), and the two pages represent a homologous pair of duplicated chromosomes. Count the number of chromosomes again. It is still equal to twice your number of students since the sister chromatids (e.g., the two left feet on one page) are still together. Students may write their initials inside each foot outline along with the letters L or R to indicate which foot was outlined.

6. Discuss events of G2 of Interphase: There's no change in chromosome number but cells may grow more and will get ready to divide.

7. Now have students walk through mitosis by keeping their feet on their papers and shuffling feet and paper across the floor.
   a. *Prophase.* Describe how duplicated chromosomes coil up and appear as x-shaped structures. Help students make the connection between their two pieces of paper and a picture of a homologous pair of duplicated chromosomes
   b. *Metaphase.* Everyone shuffles or slides their paper pieces to line them up at the equator (middle of the room).
   c. *Anaphase.* Each student must pick up and tear each page in half so, for instance, the two traced left feet are separated (same for the two traced right feet). Students place one of their separated left feet at one end of the cell while the other left foot goes to the other end. Repeat the process with the separated right feet.
   d. *Telophase.* Have students count the number of chromosomes in each new cell to see if we have the same number as in Step 4 (each new cell should have a left and right foot of each student).

For meiosis, students must "do the splits" at Anaphase I to show how homologous chromosome pairs separate, then tear pages in half during Anaphase II to show sister chromatids separating. Be sure to count chromosomes as you go.

SOURCE: Used with permission of Carol Robertson.

NOTE: It would be difficult to show crossing over with this activity; use pipe cleaner models and diagrams instead.

Preview and Preteach Critical Concepts and Vocabulary

Repetition is the mother of studies.

—Latin Proverb

Struggling readers need to hear important concepts and vocabulary explained and discussed several times and in multiple ways before they can make connections and construct new knowledge. Once is never enough. Some struggling readers also need a short preview or actual preteaching of key concepts and critical vocabulary before beginning a unit in the classroom. They may also need booster opportunities for additional practice and review once they have experienced the in-class lesson (e.g., afterschool tutoring or homework help). These opportunities increase the likelihood that struggling readers will understand and retain new information. Here are some options for achieving this goal:

1. Send home a tape player with a short tutorial on the upcoming chapter that you or another student has prepared.

2. Send home a "chapter on tape" for struggling readers to listen or read along to in advance of experiencing classroom lesson and discussions.

3. Provide easy nonfiction books based on the core concepts of your unit (e.g., cells, energy, number sense) to struggling readers. See Activity 24, Use Easy Nonfiction to Build Background Knowledge, for further ideas.

4. If available, ask a special education or remedial reading teacher or paraprofessional to give an individual or small group of students a preview of the chapter's key vocabulary and concepts.

5. Whenever possible, use photos, clip art, models, transparencies, and other visuals to illustrate difficult terms and concepts.

RECOMMENDED RESOURCE

Deshler & Schumaker, 2006. *Teaching Adolescents With Disabilities: Accessing the General Education Curriculum.*

Don't assume that this recommended resource is useful *only* to special educators. There are many struggling students in your classroom who don't qualify for special education, but could be far more successful with these approaches. See especially Chapter 3 by Deshler and Schumaker on teaching practices that optimize curriculum access.

RESEARCH ON CURRICULAR ACCESS

Afflerbach, 1990a, 1990b; Bransford, 1983; Dole et al., 1991; Pearson, Roehler, Dole, & Duffy, 1992.

Check Frequently for Understanding

Formative assessment can occur many times in every lesson. It can involve several different methods for encouraging students to express what they are thinking and several different ways of acting on such evidence.

—Black, Harrison, Lee, Marshall, and Wiliam (2003, p. 2)

The most common way for teachers to monitor students' understanding during class is to ask, "Are there any questions?" Rarely are confused students able to articulate the nature of their confusion quickly enough to respond, even if they were confident enough to show their ignorance in front of peers. Hearing no questions, the teacher could well assume that everyone gets it.

A better question to ask is, "What are your questions?" Phrasing it this way gives students the impression that there will always be questions, no matter how effectively you have taught. Once the question has been posed, be sure to provide ample wait time. See Activity 36, Increase Wait Time, for some helpful guidelines regarding how long to wait before moving on.

Here are some additional ways to check for understanding that will include all students and give you more information about how to modify instruction.

- Students respond chorally (teacher notes the percentage of students who respond incorrectly and addresses those who don't).

- Students indicate their choice for the correct answer to a question from one of two or more possible answers by holding up prepared color-coded cards. Students display one of two response cards: Yes or No.
- Students display nonverbal signals, such as thumbs up–thumbs down or arms crossed–arms uncrossed, to indicate their choice of true or false regarding the correctness of a statement.
- Students fold a piece of plain paper into fourths, using each of the eight sections (front and back of paper) to write responses and then hold them up for the teacher to see.
- Students pair with a partner and quietly explain a concept or process to each other while the teacher circulates and listens. Numbered Heads is a version of pairing in which students are permanently numbered one or two and the teacher gives a direction such as, "Ones tell Twos what an inherited trait is," or "Twos tell Ones why you think Jefferson sent Lewis and Clark to explore the West."
- Students write a question about the concept under discussion to ask a partner and then all students turn in those questions that could not be answered so the teacher can address them.
- Students keep a journal or learning log in which they write entries on each lesson in a particular unit.
- Students write their answers to questions or problems on whiteboards and hold them up for the teacher to see.
- Students place a sticky arrow or flag on the part of the story that answers the question.

RECOMMENDED RESOURCE

Black et al., 2003. *Assessment for Learning: Putting It Into Practice.*

RESEARCH ON ASSESSMENT

Reeves, 2004.

Assess for Learning *and* for Grading

Formative assessment is a process in which information about learning is evoked and then used to modify the teaching and learning activities in which teachers and students are engaged.

—Black et al. (2003, p. 122)

Teachers regularly assess students for the purpose of reporting their progress to parents. Unfortunately this mandated quarterly assessment does little to increase students' motivation to learn. In addition to collecting grades for reporting to parents, *also* assess students for how well they are learning, (1) to determine and then communicate to them the immediate status of their progress so they can take steps to improve their work products and (2) to gain information regarding how to adjust your instruction.

The power of formative assessment to increase learning and achievement lies in the immediacy of its impact on your teaching as well as on your students' learning. A test given at the end of a unit in order to assign report card grades unfortunately does neither and usually ends up as a self-fulfilling prophecy. When students are compared to one another at regular intervals during the semester with no opportunities for "do-overs," the competitive classroom environment in which some students win and some lose ensures that only some students will learn. Provide feedback to students so they can improve their work products and thereby achieve mastery of the content or process.

RECOMMENDED RESOURCE

Guskey & Bailey, 2001. *Developing Grading and Reporting Systems for Student Learning.*

RESEARCH ON ASSESSMENT FOR LEARNING

Assessment Reform Group, 2002; Wiliam, Lee, Harrison, & Black, 2004.

19

Use and Teach Content Vocabulary Daily

All words are pegs to hang ideas on.

—Henry Ward Beecher

Make the vocabulary of your subject matter come to life for students. You can't do it by simply handing out a list on Monday, assigning the definitions to be completed by Wednesday, and giving a test on Friday. Students will, as you know, mindlessly copy the meanings from the dictionary or glossary with little conceptual understanding. Word Walls won't magically infuse your students with a fabulous vocabulary, either.

Unless you personally bring those words to life, many students will memorize the meanings for the test and promptly forget them; others won't even be able to remember them for the test. Oh, some students may recognize them in their reading, but the solid understanding they need to comprehend the text of your discipline won't be there. The most important words to teach are those concepts that lay the foundation for entire units of study or for your discipline in general. Use these questions to help you formulate your priorities:

- What are the key concepts of your discipline?
- What words are indispensable to understanding the text?
- What words have multiple meanings?
- What are the common American idioms?
- What words are needed to take tests? (See Activity 20, Teach Academic Vocabulary.)

- What words are essential in your classroom and discipline for ELL students?

Here's how to teach words for mastery:

1. Post the words in your classroom in their syllabicated forms (e.g., math-e-ma-tics) to aid struggling readers who have a difficult time identifying and pronouncing multisyllabic words.

2. Provide a student-friendly definition of the word.

3. Suggest synonyms or antonyms for the word.

4. Put the new word into a context or connect it to a known concept.

5. Use the new word on multiple occasions and in multiple contexts (e.g., sentence starters, games).

6. Whenever you say the word, run your hand or a pointer under the syllables of the word as you pronounce it, quickly cueing struggling readers to associate your spoken word with the written word on the wall.

7. Place several new words into a shared context.

8. Ask questions that contain the new word so students must process its meaning in multiple ways.

9. Add the new word to an already existing classroom concept map (see Activity 11, Use and Teach Concept Maps) or construct a new concept map using the new word as the foundational concept.

10. Expect pairs of students to construct semantic word maps for new vocabulary.

11. Give students extra credit points for hearing or seeing content vocabulary in other contexts.

RECOMMENDED RESOURCES

Beck, McKeown, & Kucan, 2002. *Bringing Words to Life: Robust Vocabulary Instruction.*
Stahl, 1999. *Vocabulary Development: From Reading Research to Practice.*

RESEARCH ON DIRECT VOCABULARY INSTRUCTION

Beck, Perfetti, & McKeown, 1982.

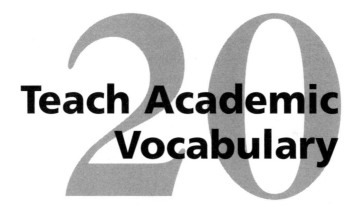

Teach Academic Vocabulary

Speak clearly, if you speak at all;
Carve every word before you let it fall.

—Holmes (1846, p. 5)

Teachers often assume that students fully comprehend the subtleties of academic vocabulary because they have been in school for years and have heard the words so many times. But do your students know what to do when they encounter academic terms in questions or directions? Not only do students need a working knowledge of the essential concepts in your discipline, they also need a solid understanding of what terms like *evaluate, discuss, explain, analyze, classify, compare, contrast, assess, outline, summarize, infer, predict, support, trace, interpret,* and *illustrate* mean. They also need to know exactly what actions or responses these terms require from them.

Some teachers create posters for the most essential academic terms their students need to know, and some teams or departments collaborate on this project to make sure that everyone is teaching the same terms and using the same definitions and examples. See Activity 19, Use and Teach Content Vocabulary Daily, for the steps to include in vocabulary instruction, and see Activity 21, Teach Vocabulary Using Graphic Organizers, for another approach to teaching vocabulary.

Consider how your students will respond to directions on a test that tell them to *trace* the events leading up to the Civil War. They may have a sound understanding of the Civil War but be unaware of the precise academic meaning of the term *trace,* thinking of another meaning (and there are at least a dozen in the dictionary). Or when they are asked to *illustrate* how poverty affects the lives of students in urban areas, they will again fall back on the meaning they learned in kindergarten.

Provide student-friendly definitions for all academic terms and when you give directions or assignments that contain such terms, model and give specific examples and nonexamples to help students take ownership of these terms.

RECOMMENDED RESOURCES

Coxhead, 2005. *The Academic Word List.*
Marzano & Pickering, 2005. *Building Academic Vocabulary: Teacher's Manual.*

RESEARCH ON ACADEMIC BACKGROUND KNOWLEDGE

Marzano, 2004.

Teach Vocabulary Using Graphic Organizers

A word, in a word, is complicated.

—Pinker (1994, p. 147)

There are four ways for students to acquire the specialized vocabulary found in content texts (Novak, 1998; Novak & Gowin, 1984): (1) hearing words explained and used in conversation and context at least three to five times (see Activity 19, Use and Teach Content Vocabulary Daily); (2) seeing words brought to life with pictures, models, and diagrams (see Activity 11, Use and Teach Concept Maps); and (3) constructing graphic organizers that show relationships between words—the topic of this approach.

Consult the I Do It, We Do It, You Do It Lesson Plan (Activity 14) whenever you introduce a new graphic organizer to students. Model the process (I Do It) by first completing an organizer like the one you want your students to eventually complete and then thinking aloud for them about how you selected the words to include in the various parts. Use a clear overhead transparency, a dry-erase board, chart paper on an easel, or Inspiration software to show your students the development of your thinking. Then give students copies of the blank organizer, select a high-interest easy word or concept, and complete the organizer together with the class (We Do It). Finally, select a concept related to your current unit of study and direct pairs of students to complete an organizer together (You Do it).

There are many graphic organizers well suited to teaching vocabulary. One of my favorites is the semantic word map. A blank form and a content-specific example can be found in Instructional Aids 21.1 and 21.2. Instructional Aid 21.3 contains a lesson template for teaching the semantic word map.

RECOMMENDED RESOURCE

Novak, 1998. *Learning, Creating, and Using Knowledge: Concept Maps as Facilitative Tools in Schools and Corporations.*

RESEARCH ON USING GRAPHIC ORGANIZERS

Novak & Gowin, 1984.

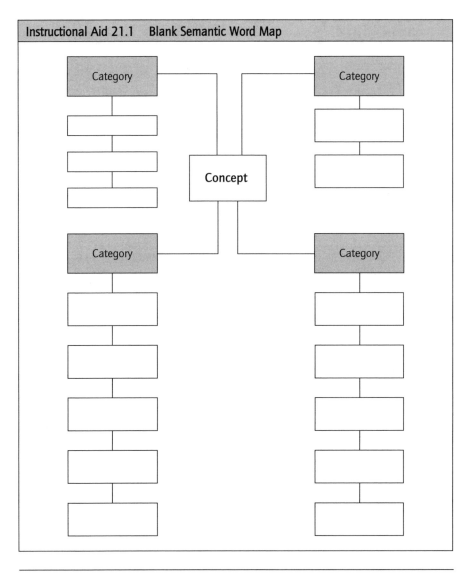

Instructional Aid 21.1   Blank Semantic Word Map

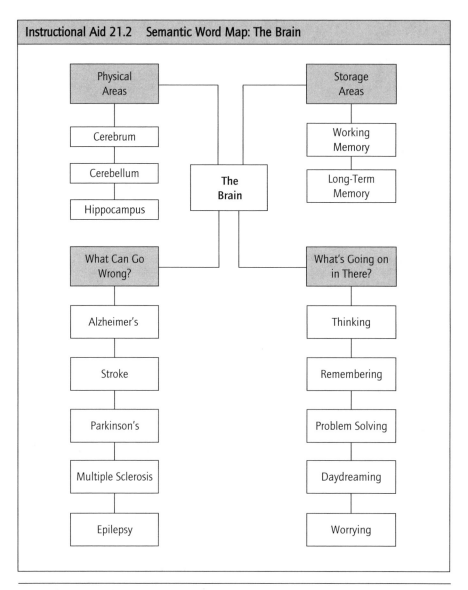

Instructional Aid 21.2   Semantic Word Map: The Brain

Instructional Aid 21.3   A Lesson Template for Teaching a Semantic Word Map

Lesson Template for Teaching Semantic Word Map	Teacher Script or Notes
1. Show students several models of semantic word maps (two well-constructed samples and two poorly done nonexamples). Explain the purpose of constructing semantic word maps and how they can be used to understand and remember the meanings of words.	
2. Introduce a key word or concept from an upcoming unit and tell students you are going to model for them and think aloud about how you construct a semantic word map.	
3. Model for students how to brainstorm a list of related words Then think aloud about how you decide which words are important and should become major categories and which words are examples of those categories. Put the words in the appropriate boxes on a large organizer on the overhead or LCD (I Do It).	
4. Choose another concept (an easy one with which students are already familiar). Activate students' background knowledge about the word by asking them to think of as many related words as they can. Then ask them to suggest categories and possible words for you to place in the appropriate boxes on a large organizer (We Do It).	
5. Choose a third concept from an upcoming lesson and ask students to first activate prior knowledge as a whole class (brainstorm a list of related words) and then complete the organizer in pairs (You Do It).	
6. Post the students' semantic word maps around the classroom and ask them to carefully review them. Debrief with students about their conclusions regarding the maps and provide time for them to add or delete items from their maps before turning them in.	

85

Reduce the Cognitive Load

The fundamental tenet of cognitive load theory is that the quality of instructional design will be raised if greater consideration is given to the role and limitations of working memory.

—Cooper (1998, p. 1)

Psychologist George Miller (1956) advanced a theory of working memory that hypothesized we can hold only about seven (plus or minus two) things in our working memories at once before we begin to get confused or forget. Because struggling students often have little prior knowledge to which they can make connections, they need to work with fewer concepts at one time until they form solid concept maps in their long-term memories. Reduce the cognitive load.

Cognitive load refers to the total amount of mental activity imposed on working memory at a specific instance in time (e.g., a classroom period or a lesson). The determinant of the weight of a cognitive load is the number of elements that need to be attended to. Students do not automatically remember what they hear or read in your classroom as if recording it on a brain equivalent of a CD or DVD. What students remember depends more on what they already know than on what you present. If the capacity of the working memory is exceeded during instruction, some if not all of the information will be forgotten. Consider modifying your instruction in these ways:

- Present only one important concept or idea at a time. For example, use a short presentation segment (e.g., 15 minutes) to introduce a new topic and then structure a processing break (5 to 10 minutes) in which students can connect the new information to something they already know, ask their classmates or teacher questions about the concept, or jot down a few key notes. (See Instructional Aid 39.7, A Lesson Template for Teaching Paragraph Structure, and Activity 37, Build In Frequent Processing Breaks.)
- Write only one critical concept on the board or overhead at a time.
- Carefully design handouts so that all of the information needed to understand or complete an assignment is on one page.
- Pass out only one handout at a time.
- Give only one direction at a time, chunk directions into smaller sections, or provide visual cues that go with each step. I have discovered that even experienced adult learners have a difficult time processing a brand-new three-step set of verbal directions for how to transition from talking in small groups to being ready to pay attention (raise their hands, stop talking, and return to their seats). When I added visual cues, most were able to follow the example of colleagues who remembered. Without the visual cues, however, participants who had moved to different places in the room would stand frozen, unable to remember Step 3. They were simply on cognitive overload.
- Eliminate the working memory load associated with asking your students to mentally integrate several sources of information by physically integrating and summarizing the sources for them.

An example of cognitive overload substantiated by research relates to animated PowerPoint and video presentations, popular techniques used by secondary teachers (Mayer, Hegarty, Mayer, & Campbell, 2005). Researchers showed that the utilization of paper-based textbooks, in which students could control the rate at which they processed the text and illustrations, led to better understanding and retention than did the use of computer-based animation and narration. Two reasons may account for the superiority of paper-based learning materials: (1) Information is presented in a more segmented and meaningful order, and (2) students can go back and forth in the printed text to find answers to questions.

RECOMMENDED RESOURCE

Paas, Renkl, & Sweller (Eds.), 2003. "Cognitive Load Theory: A Special Issue." *Educational Psychologist.*

RESEARCH ON THE POWER OF REDUCING COGNITIVE LOAD

Miller, 1956; Pollock, Chandler, & Sweller, 2002; Sweller, 1994.

Teach the Structure of Your Discipline

Expert teachers know the structure of their disciplines, and this knowledge provides them with cognitive roadmaps that guide the assignments they give students, the assessments they use to gauge students' progress and the questions they ask in the give and take of classroom life.

—Bransford et al. (2000, p. 155)

There is no one better suited to teach students how to read and write about the disciplines of science, social studies, and mathematics than the teachers who teach those subjects. Here are some questions to consider as you introduce your discipline to students:

1. How does your discipline typically present information? For example in social studies, history texts are organized in a chronological fashion. Economics and civics texts use a problem-solution or goal-action-outcome format. Geography texts emphasize description with an emphasis on comparing and contrasting various places and cultures. Science texts contain explanations of difficult concepts and complicated processes, descriptions of scientific experiments, and the juxtaposition of conflicting sources and theories (International Reading Association, 2006, p. 31).

2. How might you explicitly teach students how to read the text of your discipline? (See Activity 10, Teach Students How to Graphically Organize Text and Concepts by Chunking.)

3. What are the essential literacy skills for your discipline? For example in social studies, they include the abilities to

- Locate and use primary and secondary source documents
- Recognize and evaluate author perspective and bias
- Synthesize information from multiple sources
- Make connections across chronological eras, across geographical regions, or between civic and economic issues
- Present findings in a variety of forms, including oral presentations or debates and written documents that may take the form of research papers, position papers, or writing from a specific role or perspective (International Reading Association, 2006, p. 32)

RECOMMENDED RESOURCES

d'Ailly, 1995. "Strategies in Learning and Teaching Algebra." In *Cognitive Strategy Instruction for Middle and High Schools.*

Kobrin, 1996. *Beyond the Textbook: Teaching History Using Documents and Primary Sources.*

Myers, 1995. "Using Cognitive Strategies to Enhance Second Language Learning." In *Cognitive Strategy Instruction for Middle and High Schools.*

Their & Daviss, 2002. *The New Science Literacy.*

Woloshyn, 1995. "Science." In *Cognitive Strategy Instruction for Middle and High Schools.*

RESEARCH ON TEACHING THE STRUCTURE OF YOUR DISCIPLINE

Alexander, 1997; Alexander & Jetton, 2003; Beck & Dole, 1992; Hand, Prain, & Wallace, 2002; Shanahan, 2004; Wade & Moje, 2000.

24 Use Easy Nonfiction to Build Background Knowledge

For struggling readers, the suggestion to read an easy book, as a way to gather background information, is not filled with fear of failure or dread that the reading will take a very long time and great effort as might be the case if the assignment were to read a more difficult book.

—Pressley et al. (2005, p. 45)

Help all students—struggling readers and gifted students—to let go of the idea that reading easy books is embarrassing. Where do *you* go when you're looking for information about an unfamiliar topic? To a 400-page textbook written by experts or to an easy-reading online encyclopedia that summarizes the key concepts? Background knowledge is essential to the comprehension of more difficult text, and reading easy nonfiction that explains the critical concepts is an ideal way to expose all students to the essential background knowledge they need to understand their textbooks.

John Witmer, librarian at Alief Hastings High School (Houston, TX), believes that an excellent alternative source of concept knowledge for students whose reading levels are too low to access textbooks is a collection of easy nonfiction. He says, "My experience is that once students have been exposed to the vocabulary and concepts of academic content in easy reading material, they are more confident about making the transition to textbooks. This is especially true for ELL students" (J. Witmer, personal communication, August 1, 2006).

Seeking to develop a collection that would support math and science content and meet the needs of struggling readers, Witmer consulted with the teachers to develop a list of core concepts tested on Texas Essential Knowledge and Skills tests. John then assembled a bibliography of the best in illustrated, easy nonfiction books related to the core concepts and ordered them. He spent $2,000 on his initial collection and is ready to spend another $1,000 next year. Instructional Aid 24.1 provides a sample of John's choices.

Promoting nonfiction picture books to struggling high school readers may seem like a daunting task, but John has been creative in his approach. He explains, "I've labeled it the Parenting Collection. At least 40% of the juniors and seniors care for younger siblings, and we encourage them to check these books out to read aloud at home. We also work with parents of struggling readers to check out books that build vocabulary and concepts" (J. Witmer, personal communication, August 1, 2006). His marketing plan is working. There is a steady flow in and out of books about number sense, cells, and other high-level concepts.

RECOMMENDED RESOURCE

Carr, Buchanan, Wentz, Weiss, & Brant, 2001. "Not Just for Primary Grades: A Bibliography of Picture Books for Secondary Content Teachers." *Journal of Adolescent & Adult Literacy.*

RESEARCH ON THE ACQUISITION AND IMPORTANCE OF BACKGROUND KNOWLEDGE

Afflerbach, 1990a, 1990b; Bransford, 1983; Dole et al., 1991; Pearson et al., 1992; Pressley et al., 2005.

RESEARCH ON THE BENEFITS OF EASY READING TO BUILD BACKGROUND KNOWLEDGE

Krashen, 1989.

Instructional Aid 24.1   Selected Bibliography of Easy Content Concept Books

Title	Author	Publisher	# of Pages	Date
Adding and Subtracting Puzzles	Bryant-Mole, Karen	Usborne	32	1993
Chemistry Experiments	Johnson, Mary	Usborne	64	1988
A Drop of Blood	Showers, Paul	HarperCollins	25	2004
Energy and Power	Spurgeon, Richard	Usborne	48	1900
Forces and Movement	Llewellyn, Claire	Cherrytree Books	24	2005
The Greek Gazette	Fleming, Fergus	Usborne	32	1997
The Hershey's Milk Chocolate Multiplication Book	Palotta, Jerry	Cartwheel Books/Scholastic	32	2002
How Flowers Grow	Helbrough, Emma	Usborne	32	2003
How Much Is a Million?	Schwartz, David M.	Lothrop, Lee & Shepard Books	38	1985
Less Than Zero	Murphy, Stuart J.	HarperCollins	33	2003
The M&Ms Brand Color Pattern Book	McGrath, Barbara Barbieri	Charlesbridge	32	2002
The Magic School Bus Explores the Senses	Cole, Joanna	Scholastic Press	47	1999
Me and the Measure of Things	Sweeney, Joan	Dell Dragonfly Books	29	2002
The Medieval Messenger	Fleming, Fergus	Usborne	32	1997
On Beyond a Million	Schwartz, David M.	Dragonfly Books	32	1999

SOURCE: Reprinted by permission of John Witmer, Librarian at Alief Hastings High School, Alief ISD, Houston, TX.

Reproduction of material from this book is authorized only for the local school site or nonprofit organization that has purchased *40 Ways to Support Struggling Readers in Content Classrooms, Grades 6–12*, by Elaine K. McEwan. Thousand Oaks, CA: Corwin Press, www.corwinpress.com.

25

Determine What's Hard for Students and Teach It

Enhancing students' general knowledge is the most promising approach to enhancing their ability to comprehend what they read.

—Hirsch (2006, p. 52)

Step into the shoes (or the minds) of your students, whether struggling or gifted, and figure out what is most difficult about the text or topic you are planning to teach. Or better yet, ask them what's confusing about the topic or unit you are currently studying. With this information in hand, you can decide what approach will make the information more accessible. Even the brightest students may lack background knowledge or be confused by poorly written text. Is there too much information? Do students lack sufficient background knowledge to understand? Is the text poorly written or disorganized? Is there a great deal of unimportant information in the text?

After you have determined the most difficult aspects of your content, directly teach students what they need to know to be successful. For example, using the text, think aloud for students regarding how you distinguish between important and trivial information when you are reading. Show a video clip, draw a diagram on the board, or read aloud from a primary source document to provide background information that students may not have. If the main idea is especially difficult to understand, make a summarizing statement in advance of giving the reading assignment. Make difficult content as accessible and comprehensible as possible.

RECOMMENDED RESOURCE

Deshler & Schumaker, 2006. *Teaching Adolescents with Disabilities: Accessing the General Education Curriculum.*

Don't assume that this recommended resource is useful only to special educators. There are many struggling students in your classroom who don't qualify for special education, but could be far more successful with these approaches. See especially Chapter 3 by Deshler and Schumaker on teaching practices that optimize curriculum access.

RESEARCH ON CURRICULAR ACCESS

Afflerbach, 1990a, 1990b; Bransford, 1983; Dole et al., 1991; Pearson et al., 1992.

26

Provide Easy-to-Read Short Articles Based on Content Standards

Boiling material down to its essence and making it as clear as possible does not mean that students aren't challenged; it just means that they are challenged by the ideas instead of the presentation.

—Romer (1994)

I f you are unable to find suitable, easy nonfiction to fill your need for content-specific short text, try writing your own. This is an excellent way to guarantee that struggling readers have accessible text on topics that are essential for them to understand and retain. Who better to boil down your content to its essence than you, a subject matter specialist?

There are many commercial programs that provide leveled reading passages, but to find text that supports the specific content objectives of Algebra I, World History, or Chemistry, for example, is almost impossible. Most packaged reading comprehension programs offer passages with high-interest topics like the Loch Ness Monster or poisonous critters of the desert. However, if you teach astronomy or physics, you need short, easy-to-read passages that will help students acquire your critical content concepts. This kind of exposure to content will give them a fighting chance to answer questions on a state assessment.

If you want to try out this approach, here are the steps to writing your own passages:

1. Identify the big ideas of the chapter or unit.

2. Select five to eight key words that are essential for students to automatically and accurately identify and understand when they encounter them while reading connected text. If you are rewriting a passage from a textbook, reduce the amount of text by deleting unimportant or repeated information and collapsing long lists of items into a single word or phrase.

3. Write a passage of 125 to 150 words that includes the big ideas and uses all of the key concept words. Pretend you are talking the text to your students. Write as simply as possible. Use short sentences and a minimum of unfamiliar words, except for new vocabulary, to make the passage more accessible to struggling readers.

4. Ask a colleague to read your passage for clarity and accuracy.

5. Determine the reading grade level of your sample using an online resource like www.interventioncentral.com. Your goal is to lower the reading level of your textbook by two to three grade levels. This approach can be used in conjunction with previewing and preteaching critical concepts. See Activity 16, Preview and Preteach Critical Concepts and Vocabulary.

RECOMMENDED RESOURCE

Deshler & Schumaker, 2006. *Teaching Adolescents With Disabilities: Accessing the General Education Curriculum.*

RESEARCH ON CURRICULAR ACCESS

Afflerbach, 1990a, 1990b; Bransford, 1983; Dole et al., 1991; Pearson et al., 1992.

27

Assign Oral-Assisted Repeated Reading of Content Text

Reading research indicates that oral-assisted reading techniques, reading while listening to a fluent reading of the same text by another reader, can lead to extraordinary gains in reading fluency and overall reading achievement.

—Rasinski (2004)

Oral-assisted repeated reading uses live or taped readings of the text by skilled readers so that struggling readers can hear a suitable model and read along with the other reader. These readings would ideally take place outside of the regular school day, either as homework or an afterschool tutorial. However, to simultaneously increase content knowledge, the text chosen for repeated reading should ideally be related to your content standards.

TAPED READING

In this version of repeated oral reading, students read short passages (at their independent reading levels) aloud once or twice and then record the passage via a tape recorder. The tapes are then replayed, and students follow along with the text and monitor their oral reading. Students then record the passage again and listen for improvement. Students continue to read, record, and monitor their recording as often as needed to reach their goals.

DO YOU READ ME?

This is just another name for assisted repeated reading in which students read orally, along with a commercial or volunteer-made tape that corresponds to a selected passage or book. Some schools set up an area in the media center for what they call *automatic reading* where students read along with a tape during a study period until they can read the content passage smoothly by themselves (Dowhower, 1989).

RECOMMENDED RESOURCE

Opitz & Rasinski, 1998. *Good-Bye Round Robin: 25 Effective Oral Reading Strategies.*

Although this book was written for elementary educators, the strategies work just as well in secondary classrooms.

RESEARCH SHOWING THE VALUE OF ORAL-ASSISTED REPEATED READING OF CONTENT TEXT

Kuhn & Stahl, 2003.

28
Use a Variety of Oral Reading Approaches

Round robin reading is the outmoded practice of calling on students to read orally one after the other.

—Harris and Hodges (1995, p. 222)

If your students (or you) are bored and restless during round-robin reading, consider using an alternative that will keep them on task and tuned in. There are many reasons for eliminating round-robin reading in your classroom:

- It can cause inattentive behaviors leading to discipline problems.
- It can cause faulty reading habits instead of effective reading.
- It provides students with an inaccurate view of the reading process.
- It can hamper listening comprehension.
- It consumes valuable classroom time that could be spent on more meaningful cognitive processing activities. (Opitz & Rasinski, 1998, pp. 6–9)

The following oral reading routines provide all of the power and advantages of oral reading with none of the downsides of round-robin reading.

READ AT YOUR OWN SPEED

Consider having all students read the same text orally, but at their own speeds. It's a good way to have students get the feel of historical speeches or famous lines from literature. The din will eliminate any one student feeling singled out, and the teacher can float and encourage readers. The key to this approach is that students can set their own pace and read as dramatically or as quietly as they choose (K. Betts, personal communication, July 18, 2006).

RADIO READING

In Radio Reading, students independently practice selected portions of the text ahead of time by reading them orally as often as needed to develop expression and fluency. This type of repeated reading can be used in lieu of the teacher reading aloud to students. Small groups of students work together and prepare sections of a chapter to be read chorally. More proficient students might read parts of the chapter solo. Assign one student to act as the announcer who briefly states the purpose for reading, reads the opening and closing portions of the chapter, and also summarizes the main idea of the text (Searfoss, 1975). While reading aloud by the teacher can be helpful when text is far above the students' reading levels, Radio Reading is far more beneficial to students if the text is one they are studying as part of the curriculum.

CHORAL READING

Choral Reading is the simultaneous oral reading of text by a small group or an entire class of students. The text must be displayed on an overhead projector, or students must have their own copies. Choral Reading is an excellent way to give dysfluent students experience with more challenging text without the risk of embarrassment. I often use a Choral Reading about comprehension and the seven strategies as an anticipatory set during my workshops. (See Instructional Aid 28.1, Choral Reading: Seven Strategies of Highly Effective Readers.)

Choose a famous speech or historical document like the Gettysburg Address or the Preamble to the Constitution and read it repeatedly with the class over several days until the fluency, expression, and diction are near perfect. Then invite a guest to hear students perform before choosing another selection to prepare for performance (Miccinati, 1985).

READERS THEATER

This method of repeated reading is appropriate for English-Language Arts classes and enables students to participate in the reading of a play without the props, scenery, and endless rehearsals. Students do not memorize lines or wear costumes. They just repeatedly read their parts orally in preparation for the "performance." Play tapes of old radio shows to show students how powerful text can be when read fluently and with appropriate expression (Opitz & Rasinski, 1998).

Science teacher Carol Robertson has developed a Readers Theater presentation that tells the story of Petunia the proton and Ed the electron and the ups and downs of their relationship as they go through splitting up, rejoining briefly, splitting up again, and so on, until their final reunion in a taxi cab. The whole story takes the students through the complicated steps of the light reaction of photosynthesis. For students who have a hard time visualizing things on a molecular level, the Readers Theater approach is ideal. See Instructional Aid 28.2, Readers Theater: A Love Story—Ed and Petunia.

READ AROUND

In this method of repeated reading, students choose a favorite part of a story or book they particularly like, rehearse it until fluent, and then read it for peers, a small group, or the entire class. Students can choose poetry, narrative text, or even the lyrics of a song they particularly like (be sure to have the lyrics preapproved by the teacher). Read Around can be a required activity or offered as an optional opportunity for students once or twice a week (Tompkins, 1998). Portions of social studies and science texts or supplementary materials can also be assigned to students to practice reading aloud at home in preparation for a Read Around in class. This gives everyone the opportunity to read their assigned section several times to develop fluency, automaticity, and expression.

RECOMMENDED RESOURCE

Opitz & Rasinski, 1998. *Good-Bye Round Robin: 25 Effective Oral Reading Strategies.*

Although this book was written for elementary educators, the strategies work just as well in secondary classrooms.

RESEARCH TO SUPPORT THE WORTH OF ORAL READING

McCauley & McCauley, 1992.

Instructional Aid 28.1 Choral Reading: Seven Strategies of Highly Effective Readers

First Group:

Comprehension—the essence of reading.
Comprehension—the goal for ALL readers.
But how do we get there?
What do we do?

Second Group:

We use our brains as strategic mind tools.
We use our brains to interact with the text.
Through activating and inferring;
Through monitoring, clarifying and questioning;
Through searching and selecting;
Through summarizing, visualizing and organizing
We read strategically.

First Group:

Seven strategies for comprehension.
Seven strategies for ALL readers.
But what do they mean?
How do we use them?

Second Group:

Activating is priming the pump.
Inferring is connecting written, unwritten and the known.
Monitoring and clarifying are status checks of comprehension.
Questioning is engaging in learning dialogues.
Searching and selecting are gathering necessary information.
Summarizing is restating the meaning in one's own words.
Visualizing and organizing are creating and constructing images of meaning.
We use the strategies together to read strategically.

First Group:

Activating and inferring;
Monitoring, clarifying and questioning;

Searching and selecting;

Summarizing, visualizing and organizing;

Seven powerful strategies.

But how are they taught?

How are they learned?

Second Group:

Through thinking aloud as a master to an apprentice

With explicit models, scaffolded support and thoughtful coaching statements.

I do it–We do it–You do it.

Meaningful practice using relevant texts

Both fiction and nonfiction.

Starting simply and slowly to build success for students and teachers from the beginning.

First Group:

Think-alouds from an expert model,

Scaffolds and coaching to support learning,

Fiction and nonfiction texts relevant to the reader,

Taking time to practice, practice, practice.

I know we can do it.

I know we can become strategic.

Everybody:

Comprehension–the essence of reading.

Comprehension–the goal for ALL readers.

With seven strategies we can get there.

With powerful teaching we ALL can be strategic readers.

SOURCE: Reprinted by permission of Susan Elliott. Based on *7 Strategies of Highly Effective Readers* by Elaine K. McEwan.

Instructional Aid 28.2   Readers Theater: A Love Story—Ed and Petunia

A Love Story—Ed and Petunia

(Light Reaction of Photosynthesis)

Once upon a time, Ed (an electron) and Petunia (a proton) lived together in a water molecule inside the thylakoid membrane of a chloroplast. They were having a disagreement when Ed heard he got a promotion to PSII (photosystem II) to replace someone who got promoted to PSI (photosystem I). Petunia didn't want him to go, but he wanted the better job, so they split up (photolysis).

After Ed left her, Petunia went to work at the ATP factory and ended up outside the thylakoid membrane in the stroma. In the meantime, Ed did such good work at PSII that he got promoted to PSI. To move to his new job, he had to ride a ferryboat (proton pump) to cross the river. Lo and behold, there was Petunia sitting in one of the seats! He sat down with her and they talked about getting back together. However, they still weren't ready to resolve their differences. When the ferryboat reached the other side, Ed went on to PSI and Petunia went back into the thylakoid.

Petunia returned to work at the ATP factory and ended up in the stroma again. In the meantime, Ed got promoted once more and left PSI to go help in the Calvin cycle. At the end of his trip through the thylakoid membrane, he stepped out into the stroma to catch a taxicab (NADP+) and found Petunia getting into the same taxi! They agreed their love was stronger than before and decided to reunite at last (forming NADPH) and both go help with the Calvin cycle.

SOURCE: Used with permission of Carol Robertson.

Reproduction of material from this book is authorized only for the local school site or nonprofit organization that has purchased *40 Ways to Support Struggling Readers in Content Classrooms, Grades 6–12*, by Elaine K. McEwan. Thousand Oaks, CA: Corwin Press, www.corwinpress.com.

29

Vary Your Models, Moves, and Activities

The only person who is educated is the one who has learned how to learn . . . and change.

—Carl Rogers

Nothing piques the interest of students more than a little change on the part of their teacher. Sometimes just wearing a new tie or getting a haircut gets students' attention. But the changes suggested in this section have to do with changing your teaching models, teaching moves, and instructional activities.

Teaching models are "particular pattern[s] of instruction that [are] recognizable and consistent . . . [and have] particular values, goals, a rationale, and an orientation to how learning shall take place" (Saphier & Gower, 1997, p. 271). Models of teaching are often associated with particular theorists or researchers. For example, Roger and David Johnson (Johnson, Johnson, & Holubec, 1994), along with Robert Slavin (1990), are the most well-known scholars who have conducted research on the cooperative learning model.

Teaching moves are generic teaching actions, the things teachers do and say during instruction. There are at least 17 moves that effective teachers skillfully blend into the seamless act of teaching. A list of the moves and their definitions is shown in Instructional Aid 29.1.

Instructional activities are the plans and procedures that teachers make and follow for the purpose of instruction—the specific things teachers and students *do* during instruction. They can vary widely depending on your teaching style, your objectives, and your students. Instructional activities, when well designed, breathe life into content and make it more accessible to struggling readers. If you are in a lecturing rut, break out and try some cooperative learning (a teaching model). If all you do is talk, vow to include more thinking aloud (a teaching move) every day.

Jay Pilkington teaches middle school social studies. As a new teacher he used the lecture approach almost exclusively in his classroom. He did a lot of talking and telling, but with very discouraging results. His students weren't mastering the content, and he was stressed and exhausted. Jay wisely decided to try a new *teaching model,* a research-based one that provided opportunities for students to cognitively process the course content with classmates: cooperative learning (Johnson et al., 1994).

Jay quickly realized, however, that in order to use this popular model effectively, he would have to explain, demonstrate, and facilitate his students' mastery of the routines of cooperative learning—before he could begin teaching social studies. He also discovered that he needed some motivating *instructional activities* that fit his content, learning objectives, time frame, schoolwide expectations, *and* his students. Hoping to engage his students' interest, he came up with the three activities described in Activity 32, Create Content-Based Cooperative Games and Activities. Jay also added some new *teaching moves* to his repertoire (see Instructional Aid 29.1). He no longer stands in front of his podium talking and telling. He is now facilitating, affirming, motivating, coaching, and constructing, among other essential moves.

RECOMMENDED RESOURCES

McEwan, 2006. *How to Survive and Thrive in the First Three Weeks of School.*
Saphier & Gower, 1997. *The Skillful Teacher: Building Your Teaching Skills.*

RESEARCH TO SUPPORT THE POWER OF VARYING YOUR MODELS, MOVES, AND ACTIVITIES

Marzano, Gaddy, & Dean, 2000.

Instructional Aid 29.1	Teaching Moves
Move	*Description*
Explaining	Providing verbal input about what will happen in a lesson, what the goals are, why it's being done, how it will help students, and what the role of the teacher and the students will be during the lesson
Giving directions	Providing unambiguous and concise verbal input that seeks to give students a way to get from where they are at the beginning of a lesson, task, or unit to the achievement of a specific task or outcome; provides wait time for students to process directions, time for students to respond, and opportunities to ask clarifying questions
Modeling	Thinking aloud regarding cognitive processing (e.g., making connections with prior knowledge to something that is read in the text); demonstrating, acting out, or role-playing behaviors and actions (e.g., acting out different ways to receive a compliment given by a peer)
Reminding	Causing students to remember or think regarding something that has previously been taught; restating something that has been previously taught in a novel way to ensure remembering
Guiding practice	Leading students through a supervised rehearsal of a skill, process, or 3R (routine, rule, or rubric) to ensure understanding, accuracy, and automaticity
Scaffolding	Providing instructional support (e.g., further explanation, modeling, coaching, or additional opportunities to learn) at students' independent learning levels that enables them to solve problems, carry out tasks, master content and skills, or achieve goals that would otherwise be impossible
Coaching	Asking students to think aloud, cueing them to choose strategies that have been taught (e.g., cognitive strategies for comprehension, problem-solving strategies in math, organizational or social strategies), delivering minilessons when needed, and providing feedback to students
Attributing	Communicating to students that their accomplishments are the result of effort, wise decision making, attending to the task, exercising good judgment, and perseverance, rather than their intelligence or ability
Constructing meaning	Working collaboratively with students to extract and construct multiple meanings from conversations, discussions, and the reading together of text
Motivating-connecting	Generating interest, activating prior knowledge, and connecting instruction to the real world or the solution of real problems

(Continued)

Instructional Aid 29.1 (Continued)

Move	Description
Recapping	Summarizing what has been concluded, learned, or constructed during a given discussion or class period, as well as providing statements regarding why it is important and where it can be applied or connected in the future
Annotating	Adding additional information during the course of reading or discussion—information that students do not have but need in order to make sense of the discussion or text
Assessing	Determining both formally (through testing) and informally (through questioning) what students have learned and where instruction needs to be adjusted and adapted to achieve mastery
Facilitating	Thinking along with students and helping them develop their own ideas, rather than managing their thinking, explaining ideas, and telling them what and how to do something
Redirecting	Monitoring the level of student attention and engagement and using a variety of techniques, prompts, and signals to regain or redirect students' attention and focus on the learning task, transitioning students from one activity to another with minimal time loss
Affirming	Encouraging, praising, or rewarding students' actions, attitudes, thinking processes, verbal statements, and work products

30

Design Interactive Lessons

Passive transmission-reception of information and memorization of facts are not the kinds of learning that will be required of students for success in the 21st century.

—King (1995, p. 20)

Lessons that are well organized and briskly paced keep struggling readers engaged and on task. The recommended resource for this section (Harmin, 1994) is a treasure trove of ideas for developing academic routines that engage students. My favorite is Write-Share-Learn. It's an ideal way to activate students' prior learning and experience (see Activity 3, Teach Students How to Activate Prior Knowledge and Make Connections to New Knowledge) as well as engage and motivate struggling readers. Before you use this Write-Share-Learn academic routine as part of a lesson, teach the steps using Activity 14, Use the I Do It, We Do It, You Do It Lesson Plan.

Here's the version of Write-Share-Learn that I use in all of my workshops. Periodically throughout the day, participants are expected to jot down their thoughts regarding two to three questions I pose to them for the purpose of activating their prior knowledge on a topic. I give them a Think-Aloud form; the questions or topics related to our learning objectives are written on the left side of the sheet and space for jotting down answers is provided on the right-hand side. When thinking aloud in response to an issue or problem, there are no right answers, but I monitor and gently insist that everyone get their thoughts down in writing. Before using this structured Think-Aloud form, I found that many participants were unfocused during discussion, even though they had received a written copy of the questions. However, requiring that they respond in writing has improved participation and motivation 100%.

After writing, individuals pair up and exchange ideas. I encourage those who finish first to find another participant who is on the same timeline. This keeps fast finishers from becoming bored and gives them more time for sharing. Meanwhile, more reflective students do feel some urgency to keep moving but aren't forced to interrupt their thinking and writing too soon. About one minute before I'm ready to call time, I give a warning so that the pairs can wrap up their conversations. Then when everyone has shared, I give the group a raised-hand signal, and in less than three seconds, 100 people are back in their seats and ready to move on. See also Instructional Aid 31.1, Rubric for Evaluating Personal Think-Aloud.

RECOMMENDED RESOURCE

Harmin, 1994. *Inspiring Active Learners: A Handbook for Teachers.*

RESEARCH ON STUDENT ENGAGEMENT

Gabbert, Johnson, & Johnson, 1986.

31 Use the Cooperative Learning Model

Cooperative learning is one of the mainstays of my teaching. This approach gives students of varying strengths and abilities the opportunity to work together to solve problems and it's research-based—always a plus if you want to raise student achievement.

—Thomas Leighty, High School Social Studies Teacher

All students can benefit from working with partners to cognitively process important vocabulary and content knowledge. But the cooperative learning model is essential for struggling readers to succeed in your classroom. Cooperative learning differs from simple group work in two important ways: (1) Individual and group accountability are built into every activity so that all group members are required to participate and produce, *and* (2) group members are taught and then expected to fulfill certain roles during the cooperative process. If students arrive in your classroom without cooperative skills, consider using a simple activity like Scripted Cooperation in Dyads (Dansereau, 1988). In this activity there are just two roles for you to teach your students, *recaller* and *listener.* The steps in the script are as follows:

- Both partners listen to the presentation (or read the text chorally or silently) and take notes.
- One partner plays the role of *recaller.*

- The other partner plays the role of *listener.*
- The recaller summarizes the presentation orally without looking at any notes (recalls out loud from memory all the things that can be remembered from the presentation).
- The listener listens carefully to discover any errors or omissions (the listener can use his or her notes when listening to the summary).
- When the recaller is finished, the listener provides feedback to the recaller on errors, distortions, and material omitted.
- Together partners elaborate on the material presented: develop analogies, generate images, relate the new information to prior knowledge, or reformat the material. (Wood et al., 1995, p. 39)

The script keeps student partners on task and ensures that meaningful processing takes place. This activity can be used following a brief teacher presentation or after students have read an assigned portion of text.

Before you use this scripted process, teach it to your students using the I Do It, We Do It, You Do It Lesson Plan, Activity 14. You may also find it useful to develop a simple rubric to help students evaluate their own effectiveness as partners or groups and to help you as you evaluate their work products. See Instructional Aid 31.1, Rubric for Evaluating Personal Think-Aloud, the tool I use to assist adult participants evaluate their success at thinking aloud with a partner.

Many teachers use the cooperative model to engage students in the evaluation of written work products, such as summaries, concept maps, or graphic organizers. For example, each cooperative group might receive two or three summaries of a section of content text to evaluate. The summaries have been previously rated by the teacher according to a rubric that has been previously taught. Students are expected to read the summaries individually and then work together to rank them according to the rubric. They are then asked to explain precisely what made them rate each summary the way they did.

Heterogeneous cooperative groups provide all students with control over their own learning and provide struggling readers with the opportunity to work with strong academic role models. To maximize the benefits of the cooperative model, provide students with instruction in the model and your expectations.

RECOMMENDED RESOURCES

Johnson et al., 1994. *Cooperative Learning in the Classroom.*
Kagan, 1997. *Cooperative Learning.*

RESEARCH ON COOPERATIVE LEARNING

Slavin, 1990, 1996.

Instructional Aid 31.1	Rubric for Evaluating Personal Think-Aloud		
Performance Element	Level 3	Level 2	Level 1
Self-reflection	Highly aware of one's own viewpoint and value system, how it differs from those of others, and the impact it makes on one's own paradigm or performance; able to compare one's own viewpoint with others while remaining open to seeking out new ideas	Generally aware of one's own viewpoint and value system and how it impacts personal behavior; sometimes confuses reflection with summarizing the thoughts or beliefs of others regarding an idea or with merely summarizing one's personal opinions	Unaware of one's own belief structure and value system and how it impacts personal behavior
Expressing information and interaction with others	Expresses opinions clearly and forcefully without interrupting or insulting others; actively listens to others' points of view	Expresses opinions clearly and forcefully; ignores others' points of view	Expresses opinions and clearly and forcefully; interrupts or insults others
Use of time	Uses time effectively—works on high-priority actions first	Uses time fairly well but does not prioritize work	Wastes time; procrastinates, chooses to substitute other activities for the assigned task (e.g., distracting others with unrelated conversation)
Praise	Makes positive statements to others who need encouragement	Makes positive statements to others	Does not make positive statements to others
Active listening	Listens to partner without interrupting	Listens to partner; occasionally interrupts or changes the subject	Interrupts partner constantly
Nonverbal language and proximity	Sits or stands so that partner is able to hear and see; makes appropriate eye contact during conversation	Sits too far away or too close for partner to comfortably hear and see; makes infrequent eye contact	Is unwilling to adjust position to interact with another person; avoids eye contact

32 Create Content-Based Cooperative Games and Activities

We should not only use the brains we have, but all that we can borrow.

—Woodrow Wilson

Discouraged by the inability of his students to master content, middle school social studies teacher Jay Pilkington turned to the cooperative model as a way to boost achievement. However, he quickly discovered that he needed some cooperative games and activities to motivate and engage his students. Here are the three that he developed (J. Pilkington, personal communication, April, 2005).

ROW FEUD

Row Feud is a note-taking and discussion activity formatted like the television game show *Family Feud.* Jay's version is a combination of note taking, a pop quiz (everyone is required to answer one question), and spirited competition. Here's how he described the activity:

> I prepare a set of questions (five to go with the number of rows I have in my seating plan) and notes (answers and additional material I want to make sure the students have mastered) for the part

of the chapter that has been assigned as homework reading. First students write the five questions into their social studies notebooks. Then each team (row) is randomly assigned one of the five questions, and away we go.

READ, REVEL, AND REVEAL

Read, Revel, and Reveal is a cooperative learning activity in which small groups prepare oral presentations on different parts of a chapter—a jigsaw. Each group does the following:

a. Reads their assigned part of the chapter
b. Revels in the information by discussing the main points of their section and identifying the critical information that needs to be presented to the rest of the class
c. Prepares an "infoposter" that presents that information in any style they choose: outline, timeline, bullet list, chart, web, Venn diagram, or acrostic poem
d. Reveals the important information by presenting their "infoposter" to the rest of the class and leading a brief discussion

SHARE 'N' COMPARE

Share 'n' Compare is a partner note-taking and group discussion activity. Two students put their desks in "pods" facing each other. Jay describes the activity this way:

> I prepare a set of 10 questions and answers that relate to the chosen section or chapter in the textbook. The questions can be from any level of Bloom's Taxonomy depending on the lesson objectives for the day. Students have either read the chapter in class the day before or it has been assigned as homework for the prior evening. Students enter the 10 questions I dictate into their social studies notebooks. These notebooks are collected for a grade after each chapter. Our school uses the two-column note-taking strategy, so I've set up the questions in that fashion. The Partner Pods then work together to identify, analyze, discuss, and record the answers to the questions into their notes.
>
> Once students have completed this part of the process, I give them the "Lights out and Listen" signal (I flick the lights as a signal that students should immediately stop talking and listen to

me). I give the instruction to "De-pod and head back to camp." We then begin to Share 'n' Compare. This is a large group discussion of the answers students have written. I ask students to share the information their pod discovered and then I compare that with the information I found. This gives students an opportunity to check the accuracy of their notes and for me to elaborate on what I have written in my notes.

RECOMMENDED RESOURCE

Johnson, 1994. *The Nuts and Bolts of Cooperative Learning.*

RESEARCH IN SUPPORT OF COOPERATIVE LEARNING

Slavin, 1990, 1996.

Vary Your Seating and Grouping Arrangements

It is difficult, if not impossible, to separate instructional activity from the physical environmental setting within which it occurs.

—Lackney and Jacobs (2005, p. 1)

Middle school teacher Jay Pilkington arranges his classroom in five rows of four to six desks, an ostensibly old-fashioned seating plan. But Jay's utilization of this plan is flexible and functional.

Each row has a designated leader (the student in the first seat) and a caboose (the student in the last seat) who perform certain duties. He uses the five-row format, with an even number of students in each row, to support a variety of unique instructional activities, all designed to ensure that his students are actively involved and processing the content and big ideas of his subject.

Sometimes the rows break up into pairs. At other times the rows become cooperative learning teams that compete against other rows. On still other days, each row becomes a piece of a cooperative "jigsaw" as students prepare group presentations on an assigned section of a textbook unit (J. Pilkington, personal communication, April, 2005).

RECOMMENDED RESOURCE

McEwan, 2006. *How to Survive and Thrive in the First Three Weeks of School.*

RESEARCH TO SUPPORT A VARIETY OF SEATING AND GROUPING ARRANGEMENTS

Mosteller, Light, & Sachs, 1996; Slavin, 1996; Wheldall & Glynn, 1989.

34 Give Students Reasons for Reading

The sum of it all is: read what you like, because you like it, seeking no other reason and no other profit than the experience of reading. If you enjoy the experience, it is well; but whether you enjoy it or not the experience is worth having.

—Holbrook Jackson (as quoted in Gilbar, 1990, p. 73)

There are dozens of reasons to read. When I was in the classroom, I told students that they should read to keep from being bored. Of course, that reason now brings laughter from adolescents. Since the advent of Game Boys, iPods, and cell phones, adolescents are never bored. So I've had to come up with another Number 1 reason to read. It comes from that humorist and children's author, Dr. Seuss: "The more you read, the more things you will know. The more you learn, the more places you'll go" (Seuss, 1978, p. 27). This reason should be at the top of your list as a content teacher. Consider these additional reasons to read offered by Kelly Gallagher (2003; he also includes supporting information and lesson plans):

- Reading is rewarding.
- Reading builds a mature vocabulary.
- Reading makes you a better writer.
- Reading is hard and "hard" is necessary.
- Reading makes you smarter.

- Reading prepares you for the world of work.
- Reading well is financially rewarding.
- Reading opens the doors to college and beyond.
- Reading arms you against oppression. (p. 39)

Build motivational "reading reason" minilessons into your content instruction weekly. Once you have used a few of the ideas suggested in Gallagher's book, think of reasons to read science (to figure out if global warming is really a big problem), social studies (to find out just what did start the Civil War), mathematics (to master algebra so you can get into the college of your choice), literature (to experience other lives and go other places through the pages of a book), or computer manuals (to get a better job). Then turn to your students and ask them to come up with their own list of reasons for reading. Within the limits of your schedule and expectations, encourage students to read a lot.

RECOMMENDED RESOURCES

Gallagher, 2003. *Reading Reasons: Motivational Mini-Lessons for Middle and High School.*
Gardiner, 2005. *Building Student Literacy Through Sustained Silent Reading.*

RESEARCH ON THE BENEFITS OF READING A LOT

Graves, Juel, & Graves, 2004; Guthrie & Wigfield, 2000.

Develop and Use Scoring Rubrics

Sharing a scoring instrument [checklist, rating scale, or rubric] with students from the outset allows them to see the specific criteria on which their work will later be judged.

—Mertler (2003, p. 126)

Rubrics are scoring guides in which students' work products or performances are evaluated using specific, preestablished performance criteria along a continuum of excellence. When rubrics are well constructed as well as explicitly taught to and modeled for students in advance of giving assignments, they have the potential to accomplish the following goals:

1. Define in precise and age-appropriate language what you want your students to know, do, or be while they are in your classroom as well as when you send them on to the next level

2. Communicate those expectations to students in positive and empowering ways through the collaborative development of rubrics

3. Objectively assess students' progress toward meeting the academic and behavioral goals you have set forth and provide helpful information for modifying your instruction

4. Provide students with ongoing opportunities to self-assess their own academic, social, and behavioral progress

5. Teach your students not only the *what* but also the *how* and *why* in more explicit, systematic, and supportive ways (McEwan, 2006, p. 96)

Rubrics are even more powerful when developed in collaboration with colleagues to align student expectations across departments or with your students to empower them and increase their achievement motivation. The rubrics in Instructional Aids 35.1 through 35.3 were developed by the content departments at Alief Hastings High School (Houston, TX) as part of their schoolwide initiative to integrate literacy strategies across the content areas.

RECOMMENDED RESOURCES

Arter & McTighe, 2001. *Scoring Rubrics in the Classroom: Using Performance Criteria for Assessing and Improving Student Performance.*
Mertler, 2003. *Classroom Assessment: A Practical Guide for Educators.*
The Rubricator™ (New Measure, 2005) is a software program that speeds up the rubric design process.

RESEARCH ON THE POWER OF USING RUBRICS

Andrade, 2001; Reeves, 2004.

Instructional Aid 35.1   GROK Sheet

Name: _____   Concept: _____

Date: _____

+

1. Answer the questions.
   What did I understand?
   What is main idea?

2. Support (from lesson, article, problem)

3. What does this mean?

4. Why is this important?

GROK

To grok (pronounced GRAHK) is to understand something so well that it is fully absorbed into oneself. In Robert Heinlein's (1961) science fiction novel, *Stranger in a Strange Land*, the word is Martian and literally means "to drink" but metaphorically means "to take it all in, to understand fully, or to be at one with." Today, grok sometimes is used to include acceptance as well as comprehension (Whatis.com, 2007).

1. What didn't I understand about the lesson, problem, or article?

2. Why do I think I didn't understand it? Why am I confused?

3. What can I do to help myself?

−

SOURCE: Reprinted by permission of the Mathematics Department, Alief Hastings High School, Alief ISD, Houston, TX, and Raymond Lowery, Associate Principal.

Instructional Aid 35.2 Scoring Rubric for the GROK Sheet	
+ *Rubric*	− *Rubric*
Scorepoint 0 • Nothing written or • Too vague • Too general	**Scorepoint 0** • Nothing written or • Too vague • Too general
Scorepoint 1 • Student attempts to answer the question/demonstrate an understanding	**Scorepoint 1** • Student attempts to answer the question/explain confusion
Scorepoint 2 • Student answers the question and supports the answer with information from the lesson, article or lecture	**Scorepoint 2** • Student explains his confusion or what led to the confusion and gives examples of and details about what he or she doesn't understand
Scorepoint 3 • Student clearly answers the question, supports the answer and extends/applies/explains the importance/relevance of the information/concept in complete sentences	**Scorepoint 3** • Student clearly explains confusion or what led to confusion, gives examples of what he or she doesn't understand, and states in complete sentences the goals/solutions/actions he or she will take to clear up the confusion

SOURCE: Reprinted by permission of the Mathematics Department, Alief Hastings High School, Alief ISD, Houston, TX, and Raymond Lowery, Associate Principal.

Instructional Aid 35.3   Rubric for Social Studies Writing

Scorepoint 5

A—Excellent

In this type of response, the student . . .

- Gives a clear answer to the question
- Clearly and accurately explains/analyzes the answer
- Supports the explanation/analysis with evidence from the text that is clearly connected to the answer
- Shows a deep understanding of the event/topic throughout the answer and gives a thoughtful response when providing his or her "insight" (which answers "so what?") that is well-written, focused, and cohesive.

Scorepoint 4

B—Good

In this type of response, the student . . .

- Gives a clear answer to the question
- Clearly and accurately explains/analyzes the answer
- Supports the explanation/analysis with evidence from the text that is clearly connected to the answer
- Shows a definite understanding of the event/topic when providing his or her "insight."

Scorepoint 3

C—Good Enough

In this type of response, the student . . .

- Answers the question
- Provides an explanation/analysis
- Supports answer with evidence from the text that relates to the answer, but may not be specific
- Shows a basic understanding of the event/topic when providing his or her "insight."

Scorepoint 2

D—Almost

In this type of response, the student . . .

- Answers the question
- Provides vague explanation/analysis
- Supports with evidence that is too general, or vague, or doesn't clearly connect to the answer
- Shows little understanding of the event/topic; merely summarizes what he or she has already written; or simply restates his or her answer.

(Continued)

Instructional Aid 35.3 (Continued)

Scorepoint 1

F—Not Quite

In this type of response, the student . . .

- Answers the question in a vague or general way that shows a lack of understanding
- Provides explanation/analysis that is too general or vague
- Supports with evidence that is too general or vague and doesn't relate to the event/topic
- Shows no evidence of understanding.

Scorepoint 0

F—Nope

In this type of response, the student . . .

- Offers little attempt to answer the question, or no response at all.

Grading Scale and Point Conversions for Written Responses

Letter Scorepoint Grade	10-Point Scale	15-Point Scale	20-Point Scale	25-Point Scale	33-Point Scale	50-Point Scale	100-Point Scale	
5	9–10	14–15	18–20	23–25	30–33	45–50	90–100	A
4	7–8	12–13	16–17	20–22	27–29	40–44	80–89	B
3	7	11	15	19	25–26	37–39	75–79	C
2	6	10	14	18	23–24	35–36	70–74	D
1	5	7–9	10–13	12–17	17–22	25–34	50–69	F
0	<5	<7	<10	<12	<17	<25	<50	0

SOURCE: Reprinted by permission of the Social Studies Department, Alief Hastings High School, Alief ISD, Houston, TX; Andy McBurney, Social Studies Specialist; and Allyson Burnett, Interventionist.

Increase
Wait Time

Increasing waiting time after asking questions proved difficult to start with—due to my habitual desire to "add" something almost immediately after asking the original question. . . . Given more thinking time, students seemed to realize that a more thoughtful answer was required.

—Derek (a teacher quoted in Black et al., 2003, p. 33)

The term *wait time* was coined by Rowe (1974) and refers to the interval of silence between teachers' questions and the responses that they or their students provide to those questions. Rowe found that most teachers waited less than a second for students to respond before getting anxious and filling the dead air time with responses of their own. Research has shown that if you can wait out the silence for at least three seconds, you will see the following benefits:

- The length and correctness of students' responses will increase.
- Students will be far less likely to shrug their shoulders and respond with "I don't know" responses.
- More students will volunteer appropriate answers over time.
- Scores of students on academic achievement tests will tend to increase over time.

Stahl (1994) prefers the term *think time* and defines it as a "distinct period of uninterrupted silence by the teacher and all students so that they both can complete appropriate information processing tasks" (p. 2). To achieve the foregoing benefits, begin by explicitly teaching your students the purpose of think time, articulating your expectations for what all students should be doing during this very brief period. Unless students know ahead of time what the purpose of the silence is—to increase the likelihood that they will engage in cognitive processing as they reflect on a question—they will no doubt experience extreme discomfort when you extend your wait time longer than a second. Teach your behavioral expectations in advance if you want wait time to be productive. Model and role-play both examples and nonexamples of productive think time and then get ready to wait. Once you have mastered waiting for students to answer the questions you've posed, try another version: wait time II (Walsh & Sattes, 2004), the time you wait *after* an answer has been given so that students can process it.

RECOMMENDED RESOURCE

Stahl, 1994. *Using "Think-Time" and "Wait-Time" Skillfully in the Classroom.*

RESEARCH SUPPORTING THE WORTH OF GIVING STUDENTS TIME TO THINK

Atwood & Wilen, 1991; Tobin, 1987.

Build In Frequent Processing Breaks

There is a form of abuse occurring. Not physical or emotional abuse, but abuse nonetheless—abuse of the block. The 90-minute lecture is a form of torture for high school kids.

—Allyson Burnett, High School Interventionist

Teachers love to talk. Once we get wound up presenting on a topic we love, little can derail us. If we only knew how little most students actually retain from our pontificating, perhaps we would do far less talking. In order for meaningful learning to take place, students must cognitively process at regular intervals during a class period. Our soft-wired brains have what cognitive scientists call *activity-dependent neuroplasticity.* This means that you have the power to alter certain parts of your students' brains by giving them multiple opportunities during a lesson to actively engage those brains (Thernstrom, 2006). Cognitive processing involves writing, talking with classmates, asking and answering questions, visualizing and then drawing a picture, role-playing or acting out a process, building a model, or constructing a graphic organizer.

In the early 1990s, the typical secondary classrooms looked like this:

- Teacher talks (lectures).
- Students "listen."
- Teacher asks questions to see if students are really listening.
- Teacher's questions are of the recall type, with 20% of the questions requiring only a "yes" or "no" answer.
- Students don't interact with each other. (Tharp & Gallimore, 1991)

With the shift to a student-centered philosophy at the middle school level and block scheduling in many high schools, teachers have increased opportunities to build in processing activities.

Here are some examples from current practitioners. Marty Pope, high school English teacher, understands the importance of providing frequent opportunities for his students to process what they hear or read. Here's how he describes his routine: "After every 10 minutes of instruction, I provide two minutes for my students to reflect on and process the information. 'The reflection can be written or shared with a neighbor. What are the three most important points I just made? Turn to your neighbor and discuss.' Or 'Jot down the point you do not agree with.' This helps students to remain engaged in what we're doing without my having to continually remind them to pay attention" (M. Pope, personal communication, March, 2005).

High school science teacher Carol Robertson, who teaches in a block schedule (one and a half hours of class) advises,

> Be ready to shift gears fairly often in class. Ten to fifteen minutes is usually the maximum amount of time I spend on one topic before shifting to another activity. I specifically build in several different ways for students to process the same information.
>
> For example, when learning DNA structure, students construct a model of DNA from pipe cleaners. They then color a DNA diagram using the color scheme found on their pipe cleaner model. We also use body modeling (in the commons area) to show how DNA nucleotides (the basic building blocks) go together to form the DNA polymer. After this activity, we go back to the classroom, and I show an overhead of DNA structure. Then I give markers to a few students and ask them to circle a nucleotide on the overhead transparency. They then hand off the marker to other students who come up to circle a nucleotide. We keep going until all the nucleotides are circled. If necessary, I can also play musical chairs with the pipe cleaner models. (C. Robertson, personal communication, June, 2006)

Interventionist Allyson Burnett specializes in assisting content teachers to support struggling readers at Alief Hastings High School (Houston, TX). Here's her advice for planning a lesson "on the block:"

> Here is the schedule I typically use during a block period:
>
> - *20-Minute Segment.* Teach a concept to the whole group and then set up a processing activity or assignment.
> - *40-Minute Segment.* Students work in cooperative groups to generate a work product.

- *30-Minute Segment.* Students *share* (i.e., verbally report to the whole group); *debrief* (i.e., talk about the learning experience itself and reflect about what worked and what didn't in their groups); *clarify* (i.e., ask questions about the concept); or *publish* (i.e., show and explain their work product to the whole group).

Here are my expectations for what needs to happen during this period based on research showing what works in terms of student achievement. Whether students rise to these expectations is dependent on the extent of my explaining and modeling each one at the beginning of the school year.

- I expect students to work together cooperatively and collaboratively (Marzano, 2004; Slavin, 1990).
- I expect students to critique the various models that I provide (e.g., samples of paragraphs, graphic organizers, or summaries from a specific content area) using the agreed-upon class rubric. (See Reeves, 2004; Tierney, Soter, O'Flahavan, & McGinley, 1989. Also see the rubrics from Alief Hastings High School in Activity 35, Develop and Use Scoring Rubrics, and Activity 39, Schedule Writing in Response to Reading on a Regular Basis).
- I expect students to produce either a visual or written component based on the content I have presented and the evaluations they have conducted on the models. I expect to hear them explaining their thinking regarding the work they have done as evidence of authentic engagement in the task (see Schlechty, 2002). (A. Burnett, personal communication, August, 2006)

RECOMMENDED RESOURCES

Bransford et al., 2000. *How People Learn: Brain, Mind, Experience, and School.*
Schlechty, 2002. *Working on the Work: An Action Plan for Teachers, Principals, and Superintendants.*

RESEARCH TO SUPPORT THE POWER OF FREQUENT COGNITIVE PROCESSING

Bransford, 1979.

38

Use and Teach Mnemonic Devices

Mnemonics serve as an effective means to acquire knowledge which then can be used and expanded for the purpose of using that information to comprehend, make inferences and solve problems.

—Wood et al. (1995, p. 12)

You no doubt still remember one or two mnemonic devices (structured ways to remember things) from your growing-up years, especially if you took piano lessons: Every Good Boy Does Fine (EGBDF) for the notes in the lines of the treble clef.

You may be reluctant to teach mnemonics to your students, believing that rote memorization of isolated facts is outdated. However, mnemonics provide a way for students to acquire knowledge they will need for higher-order thinking. When knowledge can be automatically and accurately retrieved, working memory can cognitively process free from the distractions of trying to remember. Some mnemonics are verbal, and some use a combination of words and images.

If you have constructed a particularly useful mnemonic for remembering important material in your discipline, teach it to students. Having seen you model the process of developing a mnemonic, they can then construct their own as they organize and study new material. I can still recall the first-letter mnemonics I constructed for writing my doctoral comprehensive essay exams. I knew that the stress of the two-day exam would take its toll on my working memory and so for each of the major areas of the exam, I constructed a first-letter mnemonic device that spelled an easy-to-remember word to help me recall the big ideas. From that point, the writing was easy.

Mnemonics are especially effective for remembering principles, rules, and operations in science (Levin, 1993). For example, students learning how to multiply binomials $(a + b)$ $(c + d)$ can picture a sumo wrestling match between East and West teams that results in $ac + ad + bc + bd$. Mnemonics give students an organized way to practice new learning, and undeniably, practice makes the difference between remembering and forgetting.

Biology teacher Carol Robertson uses the acronym IPMAT (I Promised Myself a Telephone) to help her students remember the steps in the cell cycle (Interphase, Prophase, Metaphase, Anaphase, and Telophase) (C. Robertson, personal communication, August 1, 2006).

I developed the Five C's of Summarizing (see the Instructional Aids in Activity 9), a set of words beginning with the letter C, to help students remember the steps involved in constructing a summary: comprehend, chunk, compact, conceptualize, and connect.

RECOMMENDED RESOURCES

Mastropieri & Scruggs, 1991. *Teaching Students Ways to Remember: Strategies for Learning Mnemonically.*

Rose & Nicholl, 1998. *Accelerated Learning for the 21st Century: The Six-Step Plan to Unlock Your Master Mind.*

Willoughby & Wood, 1995. "Mnemonic Strategies." In *Cognitive Strategy Instruction for Middle and High Schools.*

RESEARCH SHOWING THE VALUE OF CONSTRUCTING AND TEACHING MNEMONIC DEVICES

Levin & Levin, 1990; Scruggs & Mastropieri, 1992.

Schedule Writing in Response to Reading on a Regular Basis

The benefits of . . . an emphasis on writing appear to be two-fold. First, students process information in a much clearer way when they are required to write an answer. They write to think and thus gain an opportunity to clarify their own thought processes. Second, teachers have the opportunity to gain rich and complex diagnostic information about why students respond to an academic challenge the way that they do.

—Reeves (2004, p. 190)

Expect all students to write in response to reading content text according to a regular schedule. The burning question is "How often?" The simple answer is "As often as you can." The benefits for student learning are proven. However, if you are like the science, math, and social studies teachers at Alief Hastings High School, time allocated for students to write was limited. And for teachers to develop and become skilled at using rubrics to evaluate writing in the content areas also took time. Teachers were granted the flexibility to set their own writing schedules. Instructional specialists and interventionist Allyson Burnett stood ready to model in the classrooms and help teachers develop rubrics.

It was the work of educational consultant Douglas Reeves that persuaded the Alief Hastings teachers to set goals in the area of writing.

Reeves examined a group of what he called 90-90-90 schools (90% minority, 90% poverty, and 90% passing the high-stakes test) and found that among other variables in common, the content teachers in these schools expected students to write a lot, the writing was evaluated by students and teachers with the use of collaboratively developed scoring rubrics, and teachers spent time talking about student writing and grading papers together.

At Alief Hastings, with 60 different cultures and 50 to 60 languages and dialects, there are struggling readers in every classroom. Teachers began to realize that assigning textbooks and holding class discussions was not enough to facilitate the kind of learning needed to master academic content. Lasting and deep learning only comes when students have to process the text they read by writing, whether to answer questions, infer outcomes, or summarize the essential ideas.

Ideally you need several tools before your students can write to learn:

- A rubric that has been developed jointly by the teachers in your discipline but also works in concert with other academic departments so as to build a unified approach to writing in response to reading across the school
- A template or lesson plan for teaching students how to write to that rubric with sufficient examples and nonexamples of responses in your content area
- Training in how to use rubrics and evaluate student writing and support in how to teach paragraph writing to students in science classes

Notice I used the word *ideally*. In order to experience the potential achievement boost that is inherent in writing in response to content reading, articulation and coordination must be present within each content department and throughout the school as a whole. However, if you want to begin experimenting with writing to learn in your content area, consult the rubrics developed at Alief Hastings found in Activity 35, Develop and Use Scoring Rubrics; check out the samples in this section; and begin by expecting your students to write in response to content text at least once or twice per grading period. The experts will advise you to do it once a week, but take it slow in the beginning.

Instructional Aid 39.7 contains Allyson Burnett's lessons for teaching the structure of the paragraph.

RECOMMENDED RESOURCE

Benjamin, 2005. *Writing in the Content Areas.*

RESEARCH ON THE BENEFITS OF REGULAR WRITING

Reeves, 2004; Shanahan, 2004.

Instructional Aid 39.1	Definitions for Developing a Rubric

Science Department

Definitions for Rubric

Paragraph

A *paragraph* is a collection of related sentences dealing with a single topic. An effective paragraph contains a topic sentence (the essential idea of the paragraph), unity (all ideas are related to and focused on the topic sentence), coherence (all sentences are related and connected to one another), and adequate development.

Topic Sentence

A *topic sentence* is a sentence that indicates in a general way the ideas the paragraph will develop. It is often the first sentence of the paragraph—but does not have to be. It is the most general sentence in the paragraph, and it is considered a "contract" between the writer and reader. The writer is promising to limit the discussion in the paragraph to the idea or ideas stated in the topic sentence.

Support

Support includes all ideas that are acceptable and reasonable methods a writer can use to prove his or her answer is accurate or correct. One nearly indisputable form of support is to quote direct words from a source.

Insight

Insight is a particularly thoughtful conclusion or interpretation. Insight shows a depth of understanding that goes beyond the literal or superficial—an understanding of the nuances.

SOURCE: Used with permission of Allyson Burnett, Interventionist, Alief Hastings High School, Alief ISD, Houston, TX.

Instructional Aid 39.2   Scoring Rubric for Writing in Response to Science Prompt

Performance Element	3 Points *Exemplary Work Product*	2 Points *Adequate Work Product*	1 Point *Insufficient Work Product*	No Points *Absent Work Product*
Topic sentence	Topic sentence specifically addresses the prompt, completely prepares the reader for what will be discussed in the remaining sentences of the paragraph in a defensible way, and does not overreach by including evidence and explanations that are inappropriate for a topic sentence.	Topic sentence partially addresses the prompt; prepares the reader for what will be discussed in a general way.	Topic sentence attempts to address the prompt; prepares the reader for what will be discussed in the remaining sentences of the paragraph.	No topic sentence
Supporting statements	Supporting statements provide sufficient evidence in support of the topic sentence. Includes at least two of the following elements: definitions of scientific terms, quotations, scientific principles, data, or a scientifically sound argument.	Supporting statements provide adequate evidence or proof in support of the topic sentence. Includes only one of the following elements: definitions of scientific terms, quotations, scientific principles, data, or a scientifically sound argument.	Supporting statements provide insufficient evidence or proof in support of the topic sentence. Attempts to include additional elements are incomplete.	No supporting statements
Further insight	Work contains a well-developed explanation that relates to the real world or larger context.	Work contains an explanation that only partially relates to the real world or larger context.	Work contains an insufficient attempt to develop an explanation that relates to the real world or larger context.	No explanation

SOURCE: Adapted by permission of the Alief Hastings High School Science Department and Craig Smith, Chairperson, Alief Hastings High School, Alief ISD, Houston, TX.

Reproduction of material from this book is authorized only for the local school site or nonprofit organization that has purchased *40 Ways to Support Struggling Readers in Content Classrooms, Grades 6–12,* by Elaine K. McEwan. Thousand Oaks, CA: Corwin Press. www.corwinpress.com.

Instructional Aid 39.3	Point Totals and Corresponding Percentages
9 = 100%	4 = 55%
8 = 95%	3 = 45%
7 = 85%	2 = 35%
6 = 75%	1 = 25%
5 = 65%	0 = 0%

SOURCE: Reprinted by permission of the Alief Hastings High School Science Department and Craig Smith, Chairperson, Alief Hastings High School, Alief ISD, Houston, TX.

Instructional Aid 39.4	Model Response for Scoring by Science Teachers

Title of Article: Human-Animal Chimeras

Prompt Given by Science Teacher: What is this article mainly about?

Topic Sentence

This article is mainly about chimeras.

Support

On the one hand, researchers need to study how stem cells behave inside the body and due to the risk, preferably not a human body! This will require "freedom to test in animals and thereby make chimeras." For example, scientists might make a mouse with human brain tissue. On the other hand, those who oppose these experiments are seeking support with laws that would "outlaw several kinds of chimeras" as well as the "introduction of animal cells into human blastocysts."

Insight

There is concern over the blurring of the boundaries that separate people from animals. Could the line be crossed enough to ever have a human female give birth to a litter of puppies?

SOURCE: Reprinted by permission of Allyson Burnett and Andi Malin, Alief Hastings High School, Alief ISD, Houston, TX.

Instructional Aid 39.5 How to Write a Paragraph	
### Getting Started Each paragraph expresses one main thought or idea and discusses it. Each paragraph should begin with your *answer to the question* that expresses your main point. At the end of your *answer*, ask "why?" Your *explanation* will answer the question "why." Remember—write in complete sentences!	### Sample Paragraph Structure • Answer to the Question • Explanation(s) • Evidence/Proof • Insight
### Answer to the Question This is your main point—you don't need to offer any words of justification for it—just state it. **Example** British Prime Minister Neville Chamberlain made the wrong decision at the Munich Conference.	### Remember to: **Write in Complete Sentences!** **Check Your Spelling!** **Use Third Person!** **Write Legibly and Neatly!**
### Explanation(s) Each explanation provides justification for your answer. It is with these sentences that you begin to answer the question, *"why?"* **Example (continued)** The naïve decision to let Hitler annex the Sudetenland encouraged Hitler to take over more countries. ### Evidence/Proof For each explanation, you must offer evidence or proof in order to be convincing. It is with these sentences that you answer the question, *"How do you know?"*	

(Continued)

Instructional Aid 39.5 (Continued)	
Example (continued) In March of 1939, after making President Hacha of Czechoslovakia feel "threatened and bullied," Hitler had his troops seize what was left of Hacha's country. **Insight** This is your opportunity to tell the reader what he or she should learn from what you have written. Your insight will answer the question, *"So what?"* **Example (continued)** Chamberlain, blinded by his desire for "peace with honor," should have known that giving in to a power-hungry dictator would just encourage more aggression.	

SOURCE: Reprinted by permission of the Social Studies Department, Alief Hastings High School, Alief ISD, Houston, TX, and Andy McBurney, Social Studies Specialist.

Instructional Aid 39.6 Paragraph-Writing Worksheet

Assignment: _____

Each paragraph expresses one main thought or idea and discusses it.

Each paragraph should begin with your *answer to the question* that expresses your main point.

At the end of your *answer,* ask "why?" Your *explanation* will answer the question "why."

Remember—write in complete sentences!

Answer to the Question

This is your main point—you don't need to offer any words of justification for it—just state it.

_____

_____

Explanation(s) and Evidence/Proof

Each explanation provides justification for your answer. It is with these sentences that you begin to answer the question, *"Why?"*

For each explanation, you must offer evidence or proof in order to be convincing. It is with these sentences that you answer the question, *"How do you know?"*

Explanation _____

_____

_____

Evidence/Proof _____

_____

_____

Insight

This is your opportunity to tell the reader what he or she should learn from what you have written. Your insight will answer the question, *"So what?"*

_____

_____

_____

SOURCE: Reprinted by permission of the Social Studies Department, Alief Hastings High School, Alief ISD, Houston, TX; Andy McBurney, Social Studies Specialist; and Allyson Burnett, Interventionist.

Instructional Aid 39.7   A Lesson Template for Teaching Paragraph Structure

Lesson Template for Teaching Paragraph Structure	Teacher Script
1. Provide direct instruction regarding the structure of a paragraph. (I Do It)	
a. Show students an example of content text for which a written response is required.	
b. Based on the content text shown in a., define, explain, and show models of (1) an answer to a question; (2) an explanation; (3) evidence/proof; and (4) insight. (See Instructional Aid 39.5 for examples from Social Studies.)	
2. Engage small groups of students in evaluating and ranking sample paragraphs. (We Do It)	
a. Have each group go to a station at the board. Each station has a set of four enlarged and laminated paragraphs from the scoring guide of the TAKS test with magnetic tape on the back. Place the four paragraphs on the magnetic chalk board in random order.	
b. Ask students to read each paragraph and arrange them in the order of their preference. The weakest sample should be on the top and the strongest one on the bottom.	
c. Ask students to write comments beside each one to explain their placement. Each group must reach consensus on the order they have chosen.	
d. Debrief in pairs about the process and synthesize the group's conclusions.	
3. Get into partners and ask each pair to write a paragraph on a transparency. (You Do It)	
a. Ask students to partner with someone and together write a topic sentence about the high school's state-ranked basketball team. (The sentences can be written on a sticky note and put up on the board, put it in a "hat" for a drawing, or written on a white board and held up.)	
b. Ask each pair to write a paragraph on an overhead transparency using their selected topic sentence.	

SOURCE: Used with permission of Allyson Burnett.

Reproduction of material from this book is authorized only for the local school site or nonprofit organization that has purchased *40 Ways to Support Struggling Readers in Content Classrooms, Grades 6–12*, by Elaine K. McEwan. Thousand Oaks, CA: Corwin Press, www.corwinpress.com.

Expect Students to Activate, Connect, and Summarize Daily

It is the types of processing activities performed at acquisition that are important for learning and remembering. As these acquisition activities are changed, the ability to remember follows suit.

—Bransford (1979, p. 52)

The activate, connect, and summarize routine is essential for engaging struggling readers with content. Even if the reading assignments are difficult, participating in the completion of this routine every day with the whole class will help to keep them on track. When this routine is mastered and regularly used, students will always know where they have been, where they are going, why they are making the trip, and what they saw along the way.

Here's a snapshot of the approach:

- *Activate.* Expect students to remember what they learned yesterday and where and how they filed it in their long-term memory.
- *Connect.* Expect students to make a connection with the learning objective for the day and their academic or personal lives.
- *Summarize.* Expect students to write or share with one another a keyword or phrase that describes the essence of what has been taught and learned during a class period and then explain how they plan to remember it until tomorrow.

Here's how one student responded to the Activating portion at the beginning of the class period. "Yesterday I learned what an inherited trait is—a physical characteristic I got from one of my parents. Since I was adopted from an orphanage in China, it's easy for me to understand inherited traits. I don't look anything like either of my adoptive parents because I don't have any of their genes. I've stored this information in my brain under a file labeled: My Real Parents. I think about them often."

Here's how another student responded to the Connecting portion of the routine. "The objective for the day is to understand how DNA is responsible for inherited traits in living organisms. I'm really interested in this topic because I love the TV show, *CSI*. The investigators are always talking about DNA, and until we started this unit, I didn't know much about it. After today's lesson, the whole thing should make more sense, I hope." Finally, here's how a student responded to the Summarizing portion of the routine, just before the bell rang. "Today we learned about a diagram called a *Punnett square* and how to use it to predict the traits of any children we might have. The best part of the class was pairing up with somebody and figuring out what our kids would be like if we had any together. Fortunately, this was only an imaginary exercise."

English teacher Dennis Szymkowiak explains how he and his colleagues help students to activate, connect, and summarize daily.

> All of my colleagues [at Mundelein High School, IL] and I use entrance and exit slips on a daily basis to check for student understanding and to give us information to keep instruction at the right difficulty level.
>
> Here's the way the routine works in my English classroom: I use 3" × 5" note cards (or just basic paper cut down to that size) for students to respond to the prompts I give to them. When students have a reading assignment for homework, the prompt for an entrance slip might be to write down three questions they have as a result of their reading. Questions work with both fiction and nonfiction, and they are a good readiness activity for student discussion.
>
> Quickly reading students' questions before class gives me an immediate understanding of the nature and extent of individual and group comprehension. If all of the questions are of a literal nature, a lesson I've planned at a higher level will need to be modified. Likewise, if students' questions reveal a deeper or more critical understanding, I can move the lesson to a higher level. (D. Szymkowiak, personal communication, April, 2005)

RECOMMENDED RESOURCES

Tovani, 2000. *I Read It, But I Don't Get It: Comprehension Strategies for Adolescent Readers.*

Zimmerman & Keene, 1997. *Mosaic of Thought: Teaching Comprehension in a Reader's Workshop.*

RESEARCH REGARDING THE POWER OF ACTIVATING, CONNECTING, AND SUMMARIZING

Afflerbach, 1990a, 1990b; Bransford, 1983; Dole et al., 1991.

Conclusion

The idea is not that content-area teachers should become reading and writing teachers, but rather that they should emphasize the reading and writing practices that are specific to their subjects, so students are encouraged to read and write like historians, scientists, mathematicians, and other subject-area experts.

—Biancarosa and Snow (2004, p. 15)

Secondary teachers are among the hardest working and most dedicated of professionals. They teach multiple sections of several different courses, advise and supervise, tutor after school and during lunch, and fit in collaborative teaming and professional development in their spare time. They plan lessons, write exams, and grade hundreds of papers. Regrettably, the time and effort expended on these activities don't always get results. Many students, especially struggling readers, fail and ultimately drop out of school.

I have written this book to help you support these students before they fall through the cracks. There are no easy answers. But there are some big ideas—ideas that can help you scaffold struggling readers in research-based and classroom-tested ways.

THE BIG IDEAS

- Content teachers are uniquely suited to helping struggling readers become more competent readers and writers of content—through thinking aloud and modeling their own processing of text reading and writing.
- The fact that there are so many struggling readers should not deter teachers from teaching content and having high expectations. Many struggling readers will catch on, get turned on, and begin to

take more responsibility for their own learning when they sense strong teacher support. Toss out a life preserver in the form of a new approach or method, and see who grabs on.

- The life preservers you have at your disposal are the 40 ways to make content more accessible to struggling readers.
- If you want struggling readers (or any students) to learn *and* remember critical academic content, they must constantly be engaged in a variety of cognitive processing activities.
- Struggling readers cannot learn from inaccessible lectures and textbooks without support.
- It is only by changing the quality and quantity of processing opportunities that struggling readers will begin to succeed.
- Infusing the 40 ways to support struggling readers into your content instruction will enhance your teaching effectiveness for all students.

In addition to these big ideas, there are also two small ideas—pervasive expectations that demoralize content teachers:

- You should not be expected to teach beginning reading. Teaching students to read from scratch is a job for highly skilled reading professionals.
- You should not be expected to teach reading skills or study skills or test preparation in isolation from your content.

MY GOALS IN WRITING THIS BOOK

I began writing this book with one goal in mind: to provide secondary teachers with research-based ways to support struggling readers in their content classrooms. When I finished writing, I realized that I also had a second goal: to support content teachers in their efforts to make a difference in the lives of struggling readers. There are two questions to answer with regard to taking on the challenge: If not now, then when? If not us, then who?

References

Adams, M. J. (1998). The three-cueing system. In F. Lehr & J. Osborn (Eds.), *Literacy for all issues in teaching and learning* (pp. 73–99). New York: Guilford.

Afflerbach, P. (1990a). The influence of prior knowledge and text genre on readers' prediction strategies. *Reading Research Quarterly, 22,* 131–148.

Afflerbach, P. (1990b). The influence of prior knowledge on expert readers' main idea strategies. *Reading Research Quarterly, 25,* 31–46.

Afflerbach, P. (2002). Teaching reading self-assessment strategies. In C. C. Block & M. Pressley (Eds.), *Comprehension instruction: Research-based best practices* (pp. 96–111). New York: Guilford.

Afflerbach, P., & Johnston, P. H. (1984). Research methodology: On the use of verbal reports in reading research. *Journal of Reading Behavior, 16,* 307–322.

Afflerbach, P., & Walker, B. (1992). Main idea instruction: An analysis of three basal reader series. *Reading Research and Instruction, 32*(1), 11–28.

Alexander, P. A. (1997). The nature of disciplinary and domain learning: The dynamics of subject-matter knowledge, strategy knowledge, and motivation. In C. E. Weinstein & B. L. McComb (Eds.), *Strategic learning: Skill, will, and self-regulation* (Vol. 10, pp. 213–250). Mahwah, NJ: Erlbaum.

Alexander, P. A., & Jetton, T. L. (2003). Learning from traditional and alternative texts: New conceptualizations for the information age. In A. C. Graesser, M. A. Gernsbacher, & S. R. Goldman (Eds.), *Handbook of discourse processes* (pp. 199–241). Mahway, NJ: Erlbaum.

Alexander, P. A., & Murphy, P. K. (1998). The research base for APA's Learner Centered Psychological Principles. In N. M. Lambert & B. L. McCombs (Eds.), *How students learn: Reforming schools through learner-centered education* (pp. 25–60). Washington, DC: American Psychological Association.

Anderson, R. C., & Pearson, P. D. (1984). A schema-theoretic view of basic processes in reading. In P. D. Pearson (Ed.), *Handbook of reading research* (pp. 255–292). White Plains, NY: Longman.

Andrade, H. G. (2001, April 17). The effects of instructional rubrics on learning to write. *Current Issues in Education* [Online], *4* (4). Available at http://cie.ed.asu.edu/volume4/number4/.

Armbruster, B. B., Anderson, T. H., & Meyer, J. L. (1991). Improving content-area reading using instructional graphics. *Reading Research Quarterly, 26*(4), 393–416.

Armbruster, B. B., Anderson, T. H., & Ostertag, J. (1987). Does text structure/ summarization instruction facilitate learning from expository text? *Reading Research Quarterly, 22,* 331–346.

Arter, J., & McTighe, J. (2001). *Scoring rubrics in the classroom: Using performance criteria for assessing and improving student performance.* Thousand Oaks, CA: Corwin Press.

Assessment Reform Group. (2002). *Research-based principles of assessment for learning.* London: King's College.

Atwood, V. A., & Wilen, W. W. (1991). Wait time and effective social studies instruction: What can research in science education tell us? *Social Education, 55,* 179–181.

Ausubel, D. (1960). The use of advance organizers in the learning and retention of meaningful verbal material. *Journal of Educational Psychology, 51,* 267–272.

Ausubel, D. (1978). In defense of advance organizers: A reply to the critics. *Review of Educational Research, 48,* 251–257.

Ausubel, D., Novak, J., & Hanesian, H. (1978*). Educational psychology: A cognitive view* (2nd ed.). New York: Holt, Rinehart & Winston.

Babbs, P. J. (1984). Monitoring cards help improve comprehension. *Reading Teacher, 18*(2), 200–204.

Baker, L. (2002). Metacognition in comprehension instruction. In C. C. Block & M. Pressley (Eds.), *Comprehension instruction: Research-based best practices* (pp. 77–95). New York: Guilford.

Bean, T. W., & Steenwyk, F. L. (1984). The effect of three forms of summarization instruction on sixth graders' summary writing and comprehension. *Journal of Reading Behavior, 16*(4), 297–306.

Beck, I. L., & Dole, J. (1992). Reading and thinking with history and science text. In C. Collins & J. N. Mangieri (Eds.), *Teaching thinking: An agenda for the twenty-first century* (pp. 3–21). Hillsdale, NJ: Erlbaum.

Beck, I. L., McKeown, M. G., Hamilton, R. L., & Kucan, L. (1997). *Questioning the author: An approach for enhancing student engagement with text.* Newark, DE: International Reading Association.

Beck, I. L., McKeown, M, G., & Kucan, L. (2002). *Bringing words to life: Robust vocabulary instruction.* New York: Guilford.

Beck, I. L., Perfetti, C. A., & McKeown, M. G. (1982). Effects of long-term vocabulary instruction on lexical access and reading comprehension. *Journal of Educational Psychology, 74,* 506–521.

Benjamin, A. (2005). *Writing in the content areas* (2nd ed). Larchmont, NY: Eye on Education.

Biancarosa, G., & Snow, C. E. (2004). *Reading next—A vision for action and research in middle and high school literacy: A report from Carnegie Corporation of New York.* Washington, DC: Alliance for Excellent Education.

Black, P., Harrison, C., Lee, C., Marshall, B., & Wiliam, D. (2003). *Assessment for learning: Putting it into practice.* Buckingham, UK: Open University Press.

Borduin, B. J., Borduin, C. M., & Manley, C. M. (1994). The use of imagery training to improve reading comprehension of second graders. *Journal of Genetic Psychology, 155*(1), 115–118.

Bransford, J. D. (1979). *Human cognition: Learning, understanding, and remembering.* Belmont, CA: Wadsworth.

Bransford, J. D. (1983). Schema activation—schema acquisition. In R. C. Anderson, J. Osborn, & R. C. Tierney (Eds.), *Learning to read in American schools* (pp. 258–272). Hillsdale, NJ: Erlbaum.

Bransford, J. D., Brown, A. L., & Cocking, R. R. (2000). *How people learn: Brain, mind, experience, and school.* Washington, DC: National Academy Press.

Brown, A. L., & Day, J. D. (1983). Macrorules for summarizing texts: The development of expertise. *Journal of Verbal Learning and Verbal Behavior, 22,* 1–14.

Cain, K., & Oakhill, J. (1998). Comprehension skill and inference-making ability: issues and causality. In C. Hulme & R. M. Joshi (Eds.), *Reading and spelling: Development and disorders* (pp. 329–342). London: Erlbaum.

Carr, K. S., Buchanan, D. L., Wentz, J. B., Weiss, M. L., & Brant, K. J. (2001). Not just for primary grades: A bibliography of picture books for secondary content teachers. *Journal of Adolescent & Adult Literacy, 45*(2), 146–153.

Collins, A., Brown, J. S., & Holum, A. (1991). Cognitive apprenticeship: Making thinking visible. *American Educator, 15*(3), 6–11, 38–46.

Collins, A., Brown, J. S., & Newman, S. E. (1990). Cognitive apprenticeship: Teaching the crafts of reading, writing, and mathematics. In L. Resnick (Ed.), *Knowing, learning, and instruction: Essays in honor of Robert Glaser* (pp. 453–494). Hillsdale, NJ: Erlbaum.

Cooper, G. (1998). *Research into cognitive load theory and instructional design at UNSW.* Retrieved December 8, 2006, from www.education.arts.unsw.eduau/

Coxhead, A. (2005). *The academic word list.* Retrieved December 8, 2006, from www.vuw.ac.nz/lals/research/awl/index.html

Cross, D. R., & Paris, S. G. (1988). Developmental and instructional analyses of children's metacognition and reading comprehension. *Journal of Educational Psychology, 80*(2), 131–142.

d'Ailly, H. (1995). Strategies in learning and teaching algebra. In E. Wood, V. E. Woloshyn, & T. Willoughby (Eds.), *Cognitive Strategy Instruction for Middle and High Schools* (pp. 137–176). Cambridge, MA: Brookline.

Dansereau, D. F. (1988). Cooperative learning strategies. In C. E. Weinstein, E. T. Goetz, & P. A, Alexander (Eds.), *Learning and study strategies: Issues in assessment, instruction, and evaluation* (pp. 103–120). New York: Academic Press.

Davey, B., & McBride, S. (1986). Effects of question-generation on reading comprehension. *Journal of Educational Psychology, 78,* 256–262.

Deshler, D., & Schumaker, J. (2006). *Teaching adolescents with disabilities: Accessing the general education curriculum.* Thousand Oaks, CA: Corwin Press.

Dole, J. (2000). Explicit and implicit instruction in comprehension. In B. M. Taylor, M. F. Graves, & P. van den Broek (Eds.), *Reading for meaning: Fostering comprehension in the middle grades* (pp. 52–69). New York: Teachers College Press.

Dole, J. A., Valencia, S. W., Greer, E. A., & Wardrop, J. L. (1991). Effects of two types of prereading instruction on the comprehension of narrative and expository text. *Reading Research Quarterly, 26*(2), 142–159.

Dowhower, S. L. (1989). Repeated reading: Research into practice. *The Reading Teacher, 42*(7), 502–506.

Dreher, M. J. (1993). Reading to locate information: Societal and educational perspectives. *Contemporary Educational Psychology, 18,* 129–138.

Dreher, M. J. (2002). Children searching and using information text: A critical part of comprehension. In C. C. Block & M. Pressley (Eds.), *Comprehension instruction: Research-based best practices* (pp. 289–317). New York: Guilford.

Dreher, M. J., & Guthrie, J. T. (1990). Cognitive processes in textbook search tasks. *Reading Research Quarterly, 25*(4), 323–339.

Duffy, G. G. (2002). The case for direct explanation of strategies. In C. C. Block & M. Pressley (Eds.), *Comprehension instruction: Research-based best practices* (pp. 28–41). New York: Guilford.

Feller, B. (2006, July 3). *Mindless reading seen as fundamental.* Retrieved July 4, 2006, from www.seattlepi.nwsource.com

Gabbert, B., Johnson, D. W., & Johnson, R. T. (1986). Cooperative learning, group-to-individual transfer, process gain, and the acquisition of cognitive reasoning strategies. *Journal of Psychology, 120*(3), 265–278.

Gallagher, K. (2003). *Reading reasons: Motivational mini-lessons for middle and high school.* Portland, ME: Stenhouse.

Gardiner, S. (2005). *Building student literacy through sustained silent reading.* Alexandria, VA: Association of Curriculum and Supervision.

Gaskins, I. W., Laird, S. R., O'Hara C., Scott, T., & Cress, C. A. (2002). Helping struggling readers make sense of reading. In C. C. Collins, L. B. Gambrell, & M. Pressley (Eds.), *Improving comprehension instruction: Rethinking research, theory, and classroom practice* (pp. 370–383). New York: Guilford.

Gilbar, S. (Ed.). (1990). *The reader's quotation book: A literary companion.* Wainscott, NY: Pushcart.

Graves, M. F., Juel, C., & Graves, B. B. (2004). *Teaching reading in the 21st century* (3rd ed.). Boston: Allyn & Bacon.

Guskey, T. R., & Bailey, J. M. (2001). *Developing grading and reporting systems for students learning.* Thousand Oaks, CA: Corwin Press.

Guthrie, J. T., & Kirsch, I. S. (1987). Distinctions between reading comprehension and locating information in text. *Journal of Educational Psychology, 79*(3), 220–227.

Guthrie, J. T., & Wigfield, A. (2000). Engagement and motivation in reading. In M. Kamil, P. Mosenthal, P. D. Pearson, & R. Barr (Eds.), *Handbook of reading research* (Vol. 3, pp. 402–422). Mahwah, NJ: Erlbaum.

Hand, B., Prain, V., & Wallace, C. (2002). Influences of writing tasks on students' answers to recall and higher-level test questions. *Research in Science Education, 32,* 19–34.

Harmin, M. (1994). *Inspiring active learners: A handbook for teachers.* Alexandria, VA: Association for Supervision and Curriculum Development.

Harp, S. F., & Mayer, R. E. (1998). How seductive details do their damage: A theory of cognitive interest in science learning. *Journal of Educational Psychology, 90*(3), 414–434.

Harris, T., & Hodges, R. (Eds.). (1995). *The literacy dictionary.* Newark, DE: International Reading Association.

Harvey, S., & Goudvis, A. (2000). *Strategies that work: Teaching comprehension to increase understanding.* Portland, ME: Stenhouse.

Heinlein, R. (1991). *Stranger in a strange land.* New York: Putnam. (Original work published 1961)

Hirsch, E. D., Jr. (2006, April 26). Reading-comprehension skills? What are they really? *Education Week, 52,* 42.

Holmes, O. W. (1846). *A rhymed lesson.* Boston: Ticknor.

Hunter, M. (1989). *Workshop on the science of teaching.* Carol Stream, IL.

Hunter, R. (2004). *Madeline Hunter's mastery teaching: Increasing instructional effectiveness in elementary and secondary schools.* Thousand Oaks, CA: Corwin Press.

Hyerle, D. (2004). *Student successes with thinking maps: School-based research, results, and models for achievement using visual tools.* Thousand Oaks, CA: Corwin Press.

International Reading Association. (2006). *Standards for middle and high school literacy coaches.* Newark, DE: Author.

Johnson, D. W. (1994). *The nuts and bolts of cooperative learning.* Edina, MN: Interaction.

Johnson, R. T., Johnson, D. W., & Holubec, D. J. (1994). *Cooperative learning in the classroom.* Alexandria, VA: Association for Supervision and Curriculum Development.

Jonassen, D. H., Beissner, K., & Yacci, M. (1993). *Structural knowledge: Techniques for representing, conveying, and acquiring structural knowledge.* Hillsdale, NJ: Erlbaum.

Jones, B. F., Pierce, J., & Hunter, B. (1988). Teaching students to construct graphic representations. *Educational Leadership, 46*(4), 20–25.

Kagan, S. (1997). *Cooperative learning.* San Clemente, CA: Kagan.

Kellaher, K. (2006). *Building comprehension: Reading passages with high-interest practice activities.* New York: Scholastic.

King, A. (1989). Effects of self-questioning training on college students' comprehension of lectures. *Contemporary Educational Psychology, 14,* 366–381.

King, A. (1990). Improving lecture comprehension: Effects of a metacognitive strategy. *Applied Educational Psychology, 29,* 331–346.

King, A. (1995). Cognitive strategies for learning from direct teaching. In E. Wood, V. E. Woloshyn, & T. Willoughby (Eds.), *Cognitive strategy instruction for middle and high schools* (pp. 18–65). Cambridge, MA: Brookline.

Kipling, R. (1994). *Just so stories.* New York: Penguin. (Original work published in 1902)

Kobrin, D. (1996). *Beyond the textbook: teaching history using documents and primary sources.* Portsmouth, NH: Heinemann.

Krashen, S. (1989). We acquire vocabulary and spelling by reading: Additional evidence for input hypothesis. *Modern Language Journal, 73*(4), 440–464.

Kuhn, M. R., & Stahl, S. A. (2003). Fluency: A review of developmental and remedial practices. *Journal of Educational Psychology, 95,* 3–21.

Lackney, J. A., & Jacobs, P. J. (2005). *Teachers as placemakers: Investigating teachers' use of the physical environment in instructional design.* Madison, WI: School Design Research Studio. College of Engineering. Retrieved December 8, 2006, from http://www.engr.wisc.edu/

Levin, J. R. (1993, November). Strategies instruction [Special issue]. *Elementary School Journal, 94*(2), 235–244.

Levin, M. E., & Levin, J. R. (1990). Scientific mnemonomies: Methods for maximizing more than memory. *American Educational Research Journal, 27*, 301–321.

Marzano, R. J. (2004). *Building background knowledge for academic achievement: Research on what works in schools.* Alexandria, VA: Association for Supervision and Curriculum Development.

Marzano, R. J., Gaddy, B. B., & Dean, C. (2000). *What works in classroom instruction.* Denver, CO: Mid-Continent Research for Education and Learning.

Marzano, R. J., & Pickering, D. (2005). *Building academic vocabulary: Teacher's manual.* Alexandria, VA: Association for Supervision and Curriculum Development.

Mastropieri, M. A., & Scruggs, T. E. (1991). *Teaching students ways to remember: Strategies for learning mnemonically.* Cambridge, MA: Brookline.

Mayer, R. E., Hegarty, M., Mayer, S., & Campbell, J. (2005). When static media promote active learning: Annotated illustrations versus narrated animations in multimedia instruction. *Journal of Experimental Psychology: Applied, 11*(4), 256–265.

McCauley, J., & McCauley, D. (1992). Using choral reading to promote language learning for ESL students. *The Reading Teacher, 45*, 526–533.

McEwan, E. K. (2004). *7 strategies of highly effective readers: Using cognitive research to boost K–8 achievement.* Thousand Oaks, CA: Corwin Press.

McEwan, E. K. (2006). *How to survive and thrive in the first three weeks of school.* Thousand Oaks, CA: Corwin Press.

Meichenbaum, D., & Biemiller, A. (1998). *Nurturing independent learners: Helping students take charge of their learning.* Cambridge, MA: Brookline.

Mertler, C. A. (2003). *Classroom assessment: A practical guide for educators.* Los Angeles: Pyrczak.

Miccinati, J. (1985). Using prosodic cues to teach oral reading fluency. *The Reading Teacher, 39*, 206–212.

Miller, G. A. (1956). The magical number seven, plus or minus two: Some limits on our capacity for processing information. *Psychological Review, 104*, 3–65.

Mosteller, F., Light, R., & Sachs, J. (1996). Sustained inquiry in education: Lesson from skill grouping and class size. *Harvard Educational Review, 66*(4), 797–828.

Myers, M. (1995). Using cognitive strategies to enhance second language learning. In E. Wood, V. E. Woloshyn, & T. Willoughby (Eds.), *Cognitive strategy instruction for middle and high schools* (pp. 226–244). Cambridge, MA: Brookline.

National Academy of Education, Commission on Reading. (1985). *Becoming a nation of readers: The report of the Commission on Reading* (Prepared by R. C. Anderson, E. H. Hiebert, J. A. Scot, & I. A. G. Wilkinson). Washington, DC: National Academy of Education, National Institute of Education, Center for the Study of Reading.

New Measure. (2005). *The Rubricator*™. Cedar Rapids, IA: Author.

No Child Left Behind Act, Pub. L. 107–110 115 §1425 H.R. 1 (2002). Retrieved December 8, 2006, from www.ed.gov/nclb/landing.jhtml

Nolte, R. Y., & Singer, H. (1985). Active comprehension: Teaching a process of reading comprehension and its effects on reading achievement. *The Reading Teacher, 39,* 24–31.

Novak, J. D. (1998). *Learning, creating, and using knowledge: Concept maps as facilitative tools in schools and corporations.* Mahwah, NJ: Erlbaum.

Novak, J. D., & Gowin, B. (1984). *Learning how to learn.* Cambridge, UK: Cambridge University Press.

Oakhill, J., Cain, K., & Yuill, N. (1998). Individual differences in children's comprehension skill: Toward an integrated model. In C. Hulme & R. M. Joshi (Eds.), *Reading and spelling: Development and disorders* (pp. 343–367). London: Erlbaum.

Opitz, M. F., & Rasinski, T. V. (1998). *Good-bye round robin: 25 effective oral reading strategies.* Portsmouth, NH: Heinemann.

Paas, F., Renkl, A., & Sweller, J. (Eds.). (2003). Cognitive load theory: A special issue. *Educational Psychologist, 38*(1).

Pearson, P. D., & Fielding, L. (1991). Comprehension instruction. In R. Barr, M. L. Kamil, P. Mosenthal, & P. D. Pearson (Eds.), *Handbook of reading research* (Vol. 2, pp. 815–860). New York: Longman.

Pearson, P. D., & Johnson, D. D. (1978). *Teaching reading comprehension.* New York: Holt, Rinehart & Winston.

Pearson, P. D., Roehler, L. R., Dole, J. A., & Duffy, G. G. (1992). Developing expertise in reading comprehension. In J. Samuels & A. Farstup (Eds.), *What research has to say about reading instruction* (pp. 145–199). Newark, DE: International Reading Association.

Pickard, P. R. (2005, September 14). Conjuring Willa Cather: A teacher on the magic of good examples. *Education Week, 35,* 37.

Pinker, S. (1994). *The language instinct.* New York: W. Morrow.

Pollock, E., Chandler, P., Sweller, J. (2002). Assimilating complex information. *Learning and Instruction, 12,* 61–86.

Pressley, M., & Afflerbach, P. (1995). *Verbal protocols of reading: The nature of constructively responsive reading.* Hillsdale, NJ: Erlbaum.

Pressley, M., Gaskins, I. W., Solic, K., Collins, S. (2005). *A portrait of Benchmark School: How a school produces high achievement in students who previously failed.* East Lansing: Michigan State University, Literacy Achievement Research Center.

Raphael, T. (1984). Teaching learners about sources of information for answering questions. *Journal of Reading, 27*(4), 303–311.

Raphael, T., & Pearson, P. D. (1985). Increasing students' awareness of sources of information for answering questions. *American Educational Research Journal, 22,* 217–236.

Raphael, T. E., & Wonnacott, C. A. (1985). Heightening fourth-grade students' sensitivity to sources of information for answering comprehension questions. *Reading Research Quarterly, 25,* 285–296.

Rasinski, T. (2004). Presentation on fluency. Paper presented at the Literacy Conference, Lancaster-Lebanon IU-13, Lancaster, PA. August, 2005.

Reeves, D. B. (2004). *Accountability in action: A blueprint for learning organizations.* Englewood, CO: Advanced Learning Press.

Romer, C. (1994). What good teachers say about teaching. Retrieved December 8, 2006 http://teaching.berkeley.edu/goodteachers/romer.html

Rose, C., & Nicholl, M. (1998). *Accelerated learning for the 21st century: The six-step plan to unlock your master mind.* New York: Dell.

Rose, D. (1995). Apprenticeship and exploration: A new approach to literacy instruction. *Scholastic Literacy Research Paper, 6,* 1–8.

Rowe, M. B. (1974). Wait time and rewards as instructional variables: Their influence on language, logic and fate control. *Journal of Research in Science Teaching, 11,* 81–94.

Saphier, J., & Gower, R. (1997). *The skillful teacher: Building your teaching skills.* Acton, MA: Research for Better Teaching.

Saphier, J., & Haley, M. A. (1993a). *Activators: Activity structures to engage students' thinking before instruction.* Acton, MA: Research for Better Teaching.

Saphier, J., & Haley, M. (1993b). *Summarizers: Activity structures to support integration and retention of new learning.* Acton, MA: Research for Better Teaching.

Schank, R. (1999). *Dynamic memory revisited.* Cambridge, UK: Cambridge University Press.

Schlechty, P. C. (2002). *Working on the work: An action plan for teachers, principals, and superintendents.* San Francisco: Jossey-Bass.

Schoenbach, R., Greenleaf, C., Cziko, C., & Hurwitz. (1999). *Reading for understanding.* San Francisco: Jossey-Bass.

Schooler, J. W., Reichle, E. D., & Halpern, D. V. (2004). Zoning out while reading: Evidence for dissociations between experience and metaconsciousness. In D. T. Levin (Ed.), *Thinking and seeing: Visual metacognition in adults and children* (pp. 203–226). Cambridge, MA: MIT Press.

Schumaker, J. B., Deshler, D. D., Bulgren, J. A, Davis, B., Lenz, B. K., & Grossen, B. (2002). Access of adolescents with disabilities to general education curriculum: Myth or reality. *Focus on Exceptional Children, 3*(3), 1–16.

Scruggs, T. E., & Mastropieri, M. A. (1992). Classroom applications of mnemonic instruction: Acquisition, maintenance, and generalization. *Exceptional Children, 58,* 219–229.

Searfoss, L. (1975). Radio reading. *The Reading Teacher, 29,* 295–296.

Seuss, Dr. (1978). *I can read with my eyes shut.* New York: Random House.

Shanahan, T. (2004). Overcoming the dominance of communication: Writing to think and to learn. In T. L. Jetton & J. A. Dole (Eds.), *Adolescent literacy research and practice* (pp. 59–74). New York: Guilford.

Sinatra, G. M., Stahl-Gemake, J., & Berg, D. N. (1984). Improving reading comprehension of disabled readers through semantic mapping. *Reading Teacher, 38*(1), 22–29.

Slavin, R. E. (1990). *Cooperative learning: Theory, research, and practice.* Englewood Cliffs, NJ: Prentice Hall.

Slavin, R. E. (1996). *Research on cooperative learning and achievement: What we know, what we need to know.* Retrieved July 28, 2006, from http://www .aegean.gr/culturaltec/c_karagiannidis/2003-2004/collaborative/slavin1996.pdf

Spires, H. A., & Estes, T. H. (2002). Reading in web-based learning environments. In C. C. Block & M. Pressley (Eds.), *Comprehension instruction: Research-based best practices* (pp. 115–125). New York: Guilford.

Stahl, R. J. (1994). *Using "think-time" and "wait-time" skillfully in the classroom.* Bloomington, IN: ERIC Clearinghouse for Social Studies/Social Science Education ED370885.

Stahl, S. (1999). *Vocabulary development: From reading research to practice.* McHenry, IL: Sagebrush.

Sweller, J. (1994). Cognitive load theory, learning difficulty, and instructional design. *Learning and Instruction, 4,* 295–312.

Tharp, R. B., & Gallimore, R. G. (1991). *Rousing minds to life: Teaching, learning and schooling in a social context.* Cambridge, UK: Cambridge University Press.

Their, M., & Daviss, B. (2002). *The new science literacy.* Portsmouth, NH: Heinemann.

Thernstorm, M. (2006, May 14). My pain, my brain. *New York Times.* Retrieved May 14, 2006, from http://www.nytimes.com

Tierney, R. J., Soter, A., O'Flahavan, J. F., & McGinley, W. (1989). The effects of reading and writing upon thinking critically. *Reading Research Quarterly, 24*(2), 134–173.

Tobin, K. (1987). The role of wait time in higher cognitive level learning. *Review of Educational Research, 57*(1), 69–95.

Tompkins, G. (1998). *Fifty literacy strategies step by step.* Upper Saddle River, NJ: Merrill.

Tovani, C. (2000). *I read it, but I don't get it: Comprehension strategies for adolescent readers.* Portsmouth, NH: Heinemann.

Trabasso, T., & Bouchard, E. (2000). *Text comprehension instruction: Report of the National Reading Panel, report of the subgroups* (Chap. 4, Pt. 2, pp. 39–69). Rockville, MD: NICHD Clearinghouse.

Trabasso, T., & Bouchard, E. (2002). Teaching readers how to comprehend text strategically. In C. C. Block & M. Pressley (Eds.), *Comprehension instruction: Research-based best practices* (pp. 176–200). New York: Guilford.

Underwood, T., & Pearson, P. D. (2004). Teaching struggling adolescent readers to comprehend what they read. In T. L. Jetton & J. A. Dole (Eds.), *Adolescent literacy research and practice* (pp. 135–161). New York: Guilford.

University of Washington Psychology Writing Center. (2006). *Summarizing a research article.* Retrieved December 8, 2006, from http://depts.washington .edu/psywc/handouts/pdf/summarizing.pdf

van den Broek, P. (1994). Comprehension and memory of narrative texts: Inference and coherence. In M. A. Gernsbacher (Ed.), *Handbook of psycholinguistics* (pp. 539–588). San Diego: Academic Press.

Wade, S. E., & Moje, E. B. (2000). The role of text in classroom learning. In M. L. Kamil, P. B. Mosenthal, P. D. Pearson, & R. Barr (Eds.), *Handbook of reading research* (Vol. 3, pp. 609–627). Mahwah, NJ: Erlbaum.

Walsh, J. A., & Sattes, B. D. (2004). *Quality questioning: Research-based practice to engage every learner.* Thousand Oaks, CA: Corwin Press.

Wandersee, J. H. (1990). Concept mapping and the cartography of cognition. *Journal of Research in Science Teaching, 27*(10), 923–936.

Whatis. (2007). Grok. Definition. Retrieved February 24, 2007 from whatis.tech target.com/definition

Wheldall, K., & Glynn, T. (1989). *Effective classroom learning: A behavioural interactionist approach to teaching.* Oxford: Basil Blackwell.

Wiliam, D., Lee, C., Harrison, C., & Black, P. (2004). Teachers developing assessment for learning: Impact on student achievement. *Assessment in Education: Principles, Policy & Practice, 11*(1), 49–65.

Willoughby, T., & Wood, E. (1995). Mnemonic strategies. In E. Wood, V. E. Woloshyn, & T. Willoughby (Eds.), *Cognitive strategy instruction for middle and high schools* (pp. 6–17). Cambridge, MA: Brookline.

Woloshyn, V. (1995). Science. In E. Wood, V. E. Woloshyn, & T. Willoughby (Eds.), *Cognitive strategy instruction for middle and high schools* (pp. 171–203). Cambridge, MA: Brookline.

Wood, E., Woloshyn, V. E., & Willoughby, T. (Eds.). (1995). *Cognitive strategy instruction for middle and high schools.* Cambridge, MA: Brookline.

Zimmerman, S., & Keene, E. O. (1997). *Mosaic of thought: Teaching comprehension in a reader's workshop.* Portsmouth, NH: Heinemann.

Index

CORWIN PRESS

The Corwin Press logo—a raven striding across an open book—represents the union of courage and learning. Corwin Press is committed to improving education for all learners by publishing books and other professional development resources for those serving the field of PreK–12 education. By providing practical, hands-on materials, Corwin Press continues to carry out the promise of its motto: **"Helping Educators Do Their Work Better."**

Promoting Excellence in School Leadership

The National Association of Secondary School Principals—promoting excellence in school leadership since 1916—provides its members the professional resources to serve as visionary leaders. NASSP further promotes student leadership development through its sponsorship of the National Honor Society®, the National Junior Honor Society®, and the National Association of Student Councils®. For more information, visit www.principals.org.